DECORATING FOR CHRISTMAS

136 Ideas to Make the Holidays Special

The Home Decorating Institute™

Copyright © 1992 Cy DeCosse Incorporated 5900 Green Oak Drive Minnetonka, Minnesota 55343
1-800-328-3895 All rights reserved Printed in U.S.A.

Library of Congress Cataloging-in-Publication Data Decorating for Christmas. p. cm. — (Arts & crafts for home decorating)
Includes index. ISBN 0-86573-353-8 1. Christmas decorations. I. Cy DeCosse Incorporated. II. Series.
TT900.C4D425 1992 745.594' 12—dc20 92-5358

CONTENTS

Decorating The Tree

The Holiday Table

Around The House

Gift Wrapping

DECORATING
FOR
CHRISTMAS

*Holiday decorating is
one of the most enjoyable
activities of the year.*

Decorations range from Victorian or gilded in style to whimsical. In many homes, family activities center around the handcrafting of decorations as children help make simple ornaments and trim the tree. Often these handcrafted items become treasured favorites.

Many holiday activities center around the table. For festive table settings, make handcrafted holiday table linens and centerpieces. You may want to select a garland centerpiece for the dining table and evergreen sprays for a buffet or side table.

Choose accessories to convey the holiday spirit throughout your home. Trim wreaths, garlands, and topiary trees in traditional colors or coordinate them with the decor of your home. Embellish easy-to-make Christmas stockings to create unique, treasured items. Scatter Santa sacks around the house for a festive appearance. Recapture the quaintness of a winter scene by making a tiny village from milk cartons and balsa wood.

Gift giving is an important part of the holidays. Share your creativity with personalized gift boxes and Victorian cards that are so special they will be saved for years to come. Or try some of the quick gift-wrapping ideas.

All information in this book has been tested; however, because skill levels and conditions vary, the publisher disclaims any liability for unsatisfactory results. Follow the manufacturers' instructions for tools and materials used to complete these projects. The publisher is not responsible for any injury or damage caused by the improper use of tools, materials, or information in this publication.

Decorating The Tree

TREETOP ANGEL

The traditional angel can be the crowning touch on a Christmas tree or the focal point on a mantel or side table. Made from crocheted doilies that are shaped with fabric stiffener, the angel shown here has a delicate, Victorian look. Select doilies with a center motif that can be clipped away, leaving a heading area for gathering as in step 4.

HOW TO MAKE A TREETOP ANGEL

MATERIALS

- Porcelain head, about 1¼" (3.2 cm) high; pearlescent white paint, if desired.
- Crocheted doilies, one each of 6", 12", and 14" (15, 30.5, and 35.5 cm) diameter.
- Liquid fabric stiffener.
- 18" (46 cm) length of ribbon, ⅛" (3 mm) wide, or narrow cording.
- Styrofoam® cone, 8" to 10" (20.5 to 25.5 cm) high.
- 24-gauge brass wire.
- Plastic wrap; wax paper.

1 Trim the base of the cone so the height is about 7½" (19.3 cm). Shape peak of the cone, trimming sides if necessary, so head will rest on cone. Apply pearlescent white paint to the head, if desired; this softens hair coloring and skin tone. Set head aside, and cover cone with plastic wrap.

2 Place the 14" (35.5 cm) doily on plastic wrap. Apply the fabric stiffener to doily until saturated, using rag or fingers. Place plastic wrap on top of doily; apply pressure with hands to distribute stiffener and squeeze out excess. Remove top layer of plastic; dab any excess stiffener from doily, using rag.

3 Remove doily from plastic wrap; place center of doily on peak of cone. Shape doily into a scalloped, flared skirt; place sheets of folded wax paper between doily and cone to support skirt. Push head onto cone, over doily, securing it with small amount of fabric stiffener.

4 Cut away center portion of 6" (15 cm) doily; discard. For collar, weave ribbon through heading on remaining outer portion of doily.

(Continued)

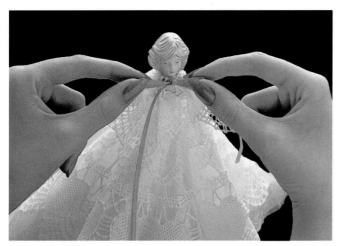

5 Place collar on plastic wrap; apply fabric stiffener to collar, except heading and ribbon, using rag or fingers. Place collar over porcelain head, and draw up heading to fit neck; secure ribbon in a bow.

6 Shape collar into soft scallops, supporting shape with crumpled plastic wrap as necessary; keep collar flat at center back to allow space for wings. Allow skirt and collar to dry thoroughly.

7 Apply fabric stiffener to 12" (30.5 cm) doily. Fold doily in half, and place on clean sheet of wax paper. Shape doily into wings, pinching center area and fanning the doily upward. Separate layers toward top of wings; stuff with crumpled plastic wrap to hold shape. Press center area flat. Allow wings to dry.

8 Remove angel from cone form. Secure collar in place with dots of hot glue. Secure the wings at center back of angel, using hot glue.

9 Cut a short length of brass wire, and shape into circle for halo, hooking ends together; secure to head, using hot glue.

MORE
IDEAS FOR
TREE TOPPERS

Unique tree toppers can be created quickly, using a variety of items. For a tree topper that holds fond memories, search through old toys or Christmas decorations for items. For an elegant yet simple look, choose silk or dried greens, spraying them with metallic paint for added glitz. Or position a bow with streamers at the top of the tree, using a special ribbon to make the bow showy and glamorous.

Twisted dried naturals, *shooting out from the top of the tree, accent a contemporary decor.*

Special toys *or stuffed animals, secured with wire to the top of the tree, personalize a toy-theme tree.*

(Continued)

Silk foliage *adds a dramatic touch to the treetop.*

Several stars, *instead of the traditional single star, are secured to the upper branches of the tree.*

Cluster bows *(page 74), wired back-to-back, make a quick tree topper. The streamers from the bows can be spiraled around the tree or tucked loosely into the branches.*

Ornaments clustered on the treetop create a focal point.

A collection of Santas adds special charm to a Christmas tree.

A single nutcracker is prominently displayed at the top of the Christmas tree.

TRADITIONAL LACE ORNAMENTS

Lace ornaments are ever-popular for a romantic holiday decor. The traditional Christmas decorations, angels and stockings, can be created in a variety of laces to make each ornament unique. Cutwork lace doilies become angel ornaments with simple folding techniques, and touches of lace trim the stocking ornaments.

HOW TO MAKE A LACE ANGEL ORNAMENT

MATERIALS

- One 4" (10 cm) and one 6" (15 cm) square lace doily.
- One 12" (30.5 cm) and two 18" (46 cm) lengths of double-sided satin ribbon, ⅛" (3 mm) wide.
- One 1" (2.5 cm) satin ball.
- 2½" (6.5 cm) strand of pearls.
- Large-eyed needle, such as chenille needle.
- Hot glue gun and glue sticks.

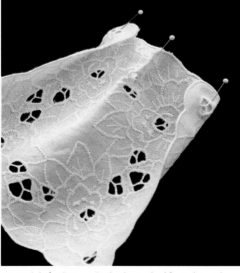

1 Fold 6" (15 cm) doily in half, right sides together; place pin ¼" (6 mm) from foldline to form tuck at center fold at one end. At sides of doily, fold ¾" (2 cm) to wrong side.

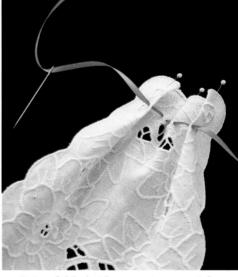

2 Bring folded sides to center on right side of doily. Thread large-eyed needle with 18" (46 cm) length of ribbon. Stitch into one fold, 1" (2.5 cm) down from upper edge; then stitch through center tuck and back up through other fold.

(Continued)

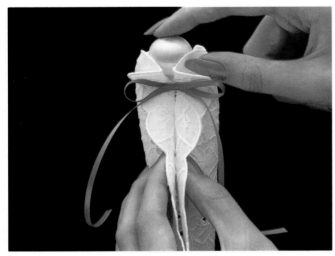

3 Tie ribbon in bow. Glue satin ball for head at top of doily, as shown, using hot glue.

4 Apply hot glue to pearls at each end of strand. Form into halo; press down onto top of head.

5 Fold 4" (10 cm) doily into ¼" (6 mm) accordion pleats; tie 18" (46 cm) ribbon around center. Tie again to knot the ribbon; tie into bow on right side of wings.

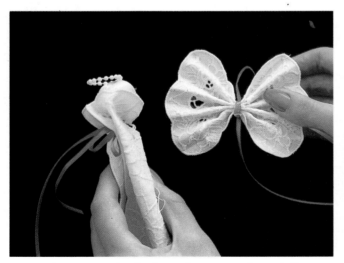

6 Apply wings to back of angel at point where doily was stitched with ribbon, using hot glue.

7 Fold 12" (30.5 cm) ribbon in half; tie ends together to make loop. Place ribbon around wings for hanger.

HOW TO MAKE A LACE STOCKING ORNAMENT

MATERIALS

- ⅛ yd. (0.15 m) fabric, such as batiste, velvet, or taffeta.
- One lace doily or handkerchief, 6" (15 cm) square or larger.
- 9" (23 cm) length of ribbon, ⅛" or ¼" (3 or 6 mm) wide.
- Hot glue gun and glue sticks.
- Embellishments as desired, such as silk rosebuds or beads.

CUTTING DIRECTIONS

- Cut two stocking pieces, using pattern on page 124.

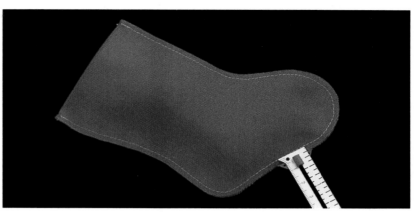

1 Place stocking pieces right sides together. Stitch ⅛" (3 mm) seam around stocking, leaving top open.

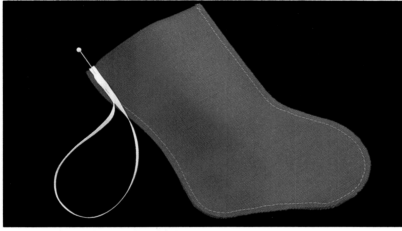

2 Fold ribbon in half; pin to wrong side of stocking, at back seam, matching raw edges of ribbon to upper edge of stocking.

3 Mark a diagonal line measuring 6½" (16.3 cm) long across corner of doily. Cut on marked line.

4 Pin corner piece of doily to the stocking, raw edges even, with right side of doily to wrong side of stocking; center ends of doily on back of stocking and corner of doily on front. Stitch ¼" (6 mm) seam.

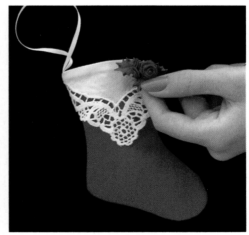

5 Turn stocking right side out, folding doily down. Secure raw edges at center back, using hand stitching. Embellish the ornament, if desired; secure items with hot glue, or hand-stitch in place.

VICTORIAN ORNAMENTS

Victorian ornaments, such as paper fans and potpourri balls, bring a touch of nostalgia to the tree. The elegant paper fans, made from paper lace or wrapping paper, and the potpourri balls, made from bridal illusion, are trimmed with embellishments for romantic appeal.

HOW TO MAKE A PAPER FAN ORNAMENT

MATERIALS

- 12" (30.5 cm) length of paper lace, 2½" to 4" (6.5 to 10 cm) wide; or 12" (30.5 cm) length of wrapping paper, 4" (10 cm) wide.
- Metallic or pearlescent acrylic paint, optional.
- 9" (23 cm) length of narrow ribbon or cord, for hanging ornament.
- Embellishments as desired, such as dried rosebuds, statice, pearl strands, and ribbon.

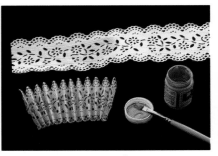

1 Apply a light coat of metallic or pearlescent paint to right side of paper, if desired; thin paint as necessary, for a transparent effect. Fold paper in ½" to ⅝" (1.3 to 1.5 cm) accordion pleats, making first fold to back side of paper. Trim excess paper at end, if necessary.

2 Glue pleats together at lower edge; clamp glued ends together with clothespin until dry. Open pleats into fan.

3 Lace ribbon through a hole in top of fan; knot ends together to form hanger. Glue embellishments at lower end of fan.

HOW TO MAKE A POTPOURRI BALL ORNAMENT

MATERIALS

- Bridal illusion, or tulle; 5" (12.5 cm) length of pregathered lace, about 1" (2.5 cm) wide.
- Potpourri, 1 c. (2.50 mL) for each ornament.
- 3" (7.5 cm) length of 24-gauge brass wire.
- 9" (23 cm) length of narrow ribbon, for hanging ornament.
- Embellishments as desired, such as dried rosebuds, statice, pearl strands, and ribbon.

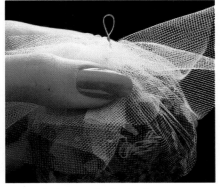

1 Place potpourri in center of 12" (30.5 cm) circle of bridal illusion. Gather illusion around potpourri to form ball; secure by twisting wire around gathers.

2 Push one end of wire into center of gathered illusion; fold over and twist to form loop. Trim excess wire.

3 Insert ribbon through wire loop; tie ends together. Glue lace around potpourri ball, overlapping ends. Add embellishments as desired.

MORE IDEAS FOR VICTORIAN ORNAMENTS

Lace balls and nosegays *are simple to make. Use lace doilies or flat lace trims for fast construction, taking advantage of the laces' prefinished edges.*

HOW TO MAKE A LACE BALL ORNAMENT

MATERIALS

- 12" (30.5 cm) round lace doily.
- 3" or 3½" (7.5 or 9 cm) clear, luminescent, or colored ball ornament.
- 9" (23 cm) length of narrow cord or ribbon, for hanging ornament.
- One or two 22" (56 cm) lengths of narrow ribbon.
- Hot glue gun and glue sticks.
- Embellishments as desired, such as baby's breath, berries, and pinecones.

1 Insert cord into ornament hanger; tie ends. Wrap doily around ball, with center of doily at bottom of ball. Tie ribbon around doily at top of ball; if two ribbons are used, tie them as one bow, and separate loops.

2 Pull edges of doily and adjust ribbons so doily is stretched to fit around ball. Embellish ornament as desired; secure items with hot glue.

HOW TO MAKE A LACE NOSEGAY ORNAMENT

MATERIALS

- 18" (46 cm) length of flat lace trim or 12" (30.5 cm) length of pleated lace trim, 1¾" to 2¾" (4.5 to 7 cm) wide.
- 9" (23 cm) length of narrow ribbon or cord, for hanging ornament.
- Hot glue gun and glue sticks.
- Embellishments as desired, such as ribbons, pearl strands, ribbon roses, and silk flowers.

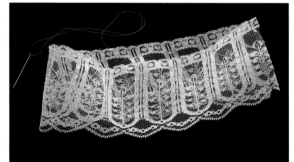

1 **Single-layer ornament.** Remove heading from lace, if pleated lace is used. Join ends of lace, right sides together, in ¼" (6 mm) seam. Then stitch ⅛" (3 mm) from upper edge of lace, using short running stitches.

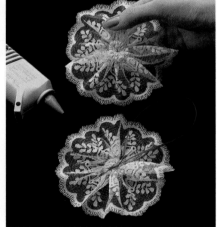

2 Pull thread, gathering lace into a tight circle; secure thread. Flatten the lace circle by pressing it gently with hand.

3 Fold ribbon in half; tie ends together to make loop for hanger. Glue loop to right side of lace at center. Add embellishments as desired.

Double-layer ornament. Make two lace circles as in steps 1 and 2; add ribbon loop to one circle as in step 3. Glue lace circles together, with loop between circles.

GILDED
ORNAMENTS

Add a touch of glitz to your tree with a variety of golden and jewel-tone ornaments. Fill clear or luminescent balls with glittery tinsel. String clusters of small sleigh bells on wire and tie them with gold-trimmed bows. Or cover Styrofoam® balls with fabric and trim them with braids to coordinate with the room decor.

MATERIALS

- Clear or luminescent glass ball with removable top.
- Shredded tinsel.
- Hot glue gun and glue sticks.

- 9" (23 cm) length of gold cord, for hanging ornament.
- Embellishments as desired, such as ribbon, statice, berries, and sprigs of greenery.

HOW TO MAKE A TINSEL-FILLED ORNAMENT

1 Remove top of ornament. Insert desired amount of shredded tinsel into ball; replace top. Tinsel may be curled, as for curling ribbon, if desired.

2 Insert gold cord through wire holder; tie ends. Attach embellishments to top of ornament, if desired, using hot glue.

MATERIALS

- Nine ⅝" (1.5 cm) sleigh bells.
- 8" (20.5 cm) length of 24-gauge brass wire.
- 10" (25.5 cm) length of ribbon, ⅝" (1.5 cm) wide.
- 8" (20.5 cm) length of ribbon, ¼" (6 mm) wide.
- 9" (23 cm) length of gold cord, for hanging ornament.

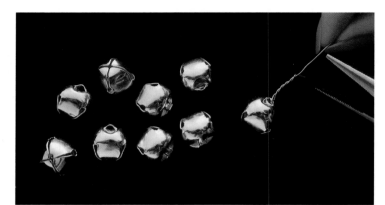

1 Insert about 1" (2.5 cm) of wire through hanger of bell; twist to secure.

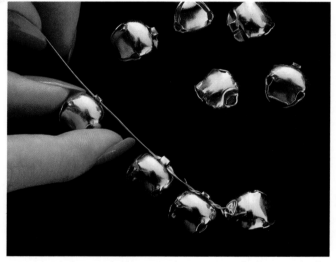

2 Insert other end of wire into remaining bells. First bell will be at bottom of ornament.

3 Make bow by folding ⅝" (1.5 cm) ribbon back and forth, forming a loop on each side; secure above top bell by wrapping wire around center of bow several times.

4 Form wire loop above bow, twisting wire to secure; trim excess wire.

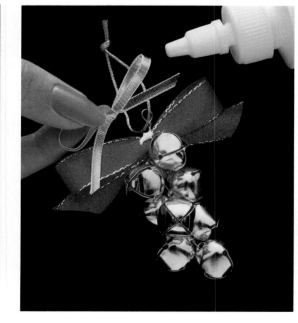

5 Insert gold cord through the wire loop; tie ends. Tie ¼" (6 mm) ribbon in small bow; glue at center of looped bow, concealing the wire.

HOW TO MAKE A FABRIC-WRAPPED ORNAMENT

MATERIALS

- 3" (7.5 cm) Styrofoam® ball.
- ¼ yd. (0.25 m) fabric.
- 12" (30.5 cm) length of gold braid, ½" (1.3 cm) wide.
- 22" (56 cm) length of gold braid, ¼" (6 mm) wide.
- 9" (23 cm) length of gold cord and decorative cap, for hanging ornament.
- One tassel.
- Fabric glue; hot glue gun and glue sticks.

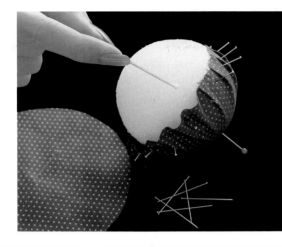

1 Cut two fabric circles, 4¾" (12 cm) in diameter; pin-mark center of each circle. Pin one circle to Styrofoam ball, distributing fullness evenly at raw edge. Glue edge of fabric to ball, making small tucks to ease in fullness.

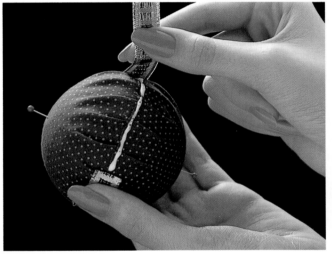

2 Repeat for opposite side of ball, using remaining fabric circle. Glue ½" (1.3 cm) gold braid around middle of ball, covering raw edges of fabric.

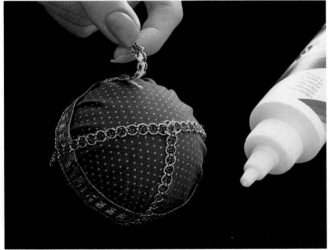

3 Cut ¼" (6 mm) gold braid in half; glue around ball in opposite directions, dividing ball into four sections. Use center pin marks as guide for centering braid.

4 Insert gold cord in decorative cap; knot ends. Shape cap to fit top of ornament; secure with hot glue.

5 Attach tassel to bottom of ornament, using hot glue.

SNOWMAN ORNAMENTS

These handcrafted snowmen are easily made by applying an artificial snow paste over a Styrofoam® form. Their fine features are shaped from polymer clay, a modeling compound that can be oven-baked. These tree ornaments can also be used to decorate packages and wreaths.

TIPS FOR SHAPING POLYMER CLAY

Work with the clay on a smooth, clean, flat surface. If the surface is porous, protect it with a sheet of wax paper or aluminum foil, secured to the surface with tape. Wipe the work surface and tools with petroleum jelly to prevent the clay from sticking.

Knead the clay to soften it with the warmth of your hands before shaping it.

Mix a dab of petroleum jelly into the clay if it seems dry. Keep your hands moist with petroleum jelly or hand lotion.

Roll the clay into balls of the desired size; use a circle gauge, available from stationery stores, to measure the balls.

Roll out the clay, using a rolling pin, to flatten it. Cut the clay with scissors or a mat knife.

HOW TO MAKE A SNOWMAN ORNAMENT

MATERIALS

- One 1½" (3.8 cm) Styrofoam ball; one 2½" (6.5 cm) Styrofoam egg.

- Polymer clay, such as Fimo® or Sculpey®, in orange, black, tan, red, and green.

- Artificial snow paste, such as Snow Accents™; palette knife.

- Small forked twigs; scrap of plaid wool; other accessories as desired.

- 24-gauge brass wire, for hanging ornament.

- Aerosol clear acrylic sealer.

- Toothpicks; wax paper; foam cup; baking sheet.

- Scissors or mat knife.

- Craft glue; hot glue gun and glue sticks.

1 Roll small end of Styrofoam egg, on smooth, hard surface to taper sides slightly. For snowmen with hats, trim a small amount from Styrofoam ball to flatten top. Insert toothpick halfway into the tapered end of the egg; place craft glue at base, and secure ball on top of egg, pushing it onto remainder of toothpick.

2 Form carrot by rolling ¼" (6 mm) ball of orange clay into tapered shape. Using scissors, cut buttons, eyes, and mouth from black clay that has been flattened; cut three larger pieces for buttons and six smaller ones for eyes and mouth.

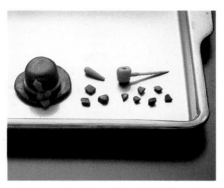

3 Form hat by flattening ½" (1.3 cm) ball of black clay into round brim. Roll ¾" (2 cm) ball into a cylinder; flatten the ends, and place on brim, pressing gently.

4 Roll the clay for red hatband and green holly leaves to 1/16" (1.5 mm) thickness; cut, using scissors. Roll small berries from red clay. Gently press the hatband around the hat, and position holly and berries.

5 Form pipe by rolling ¼" (6 mm) ball of tan clay into cylinder; insert a piece of toothpick for pipe stem. Hollow out pipe and add texture, using toothpick. Press small amount of clay around toothpick near pipe bowl. Bake clay pieces on a baking sheet until hardened, following the manufacturer's instructions; hats may require more time.

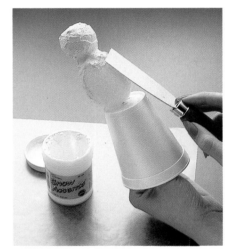

6 Apply a thin coat of snow paste to Styrofoam, using palette knife; for ease in handling, mount on an inverted foam cup, using a toothpick.

7 Press clay features in place on wet snow surface. Allow snowman to dry thoroughly.

8 Make holes for twig arms, using toothpick or blunt needle. Apply craft glue to ends of twigs; insert into holes. Repeat to insert pipe.

9 Cut fabric 1" × 9" (2.5 × 23 cm) for the neck scarf. Fringe edges, and glue scarf in place. For woman, make head scarf from 5" (12.5 cm) square. Glue on additional accessories as desired.

10 Form 8" (20.5 cm) piece of wire into loop; twist ends together. Make hole in back of head. Apply glue to wire; insert in hole. Spray the entire snowman with a light coat of acrylic sealer. Remove snowman from cup, and touch up bottom of snowman with snow paste.

DRUM ORNAMENT

This drum ornament is cleverly crafted by forming prestarched fabric over the cap of an aerosol can. Paint drums in subdued colors for a realistic look or in an array of colors for a theme Christmas tree. An oil-based stain applied over the paint gives an antiqued look.

TIPS FOR USING PRESTARCHED FABRIC

Dip fabric pieces quickly in cool water; begin shaping immediately.

Work quickly, and do not handle the fabric any more than necessary. If the fabric is overworked, it becomes limp and does not hold its shape.

Keep your fingers wet during shaping to prevent the fabric from sticking to them.

Adjust the folds of the fabric with T-pins to avoid overworking the fabric.

Allow the fabric to dry overnight, and apply two light coats of acrylic sealer before painting.

Apply two coats of paint to the fabric for good coverage, allowing the first coat to dry before applying the second coat.

HOW TO MAKE A DRUM ORNAMENT

MATERIALS

- Prestarched fabric, such as Dip 'n Drape®, Drape 'n Shape, and Fab-U-Drape®.

- Cylinder-shaped plastic cap from aerosol can, about 2½" (6.5 cm) in diameter by 2" (5 cm) high; rubber band to fit around cap.

- Acrylic paints and brushes; ivory paint for top of drum and desired color for base of drum.

- Two ⅜" (1 cm) wooden beads and two round toothpicks, for drumsticks.

- 15" (38 cm) length of cord or leather lacing; sprig of artificial holly.

- Oil-based stain; aerosol clear acrylic sealer.

- Hot glue gun and glue sticks; wax paper.

- Permanent marking pen for personalizing ornament, optional.

CUTTING DIRECTIONS

From prestarched fabric, cut one 7" (18 cm) and one 4½" (11.5 cm) square of fabric for each ornament.

1 Dip 7" (18 cm) square of fabric in cool water for 5 to 10 seconds; center fabric over top of the plastic cap. Pull fabric down over sides, smoothing folds flush against cap; fold and finger-press raw edges to inside of cap. Turn cap over; allow to dry on wax paper.

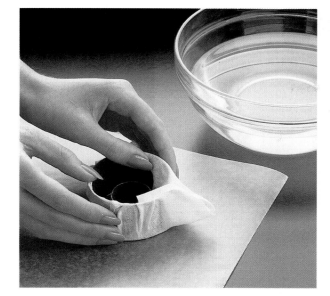

2 Wet 4½" (11.5 cm) square of fabric as in step 1; center it over cap opening. Place rubber band around cap, about ¼" (6 mm) from edge; gently pull fabric taut.

3 Fold under raw edges, working with wet fingers; leave edges scalloped. When dry, remove the rubber band.

4 Apply acrylic sealer to drum. Paint top of drum ivory; paint base of drum desired color. When dry, apply second coat; allow to dry. Apply the stain to the drum, using old brush and following the manufacturer's instructions; wipe off excess stain with soft rag. If stain reappears while drying, rewipe as necessary.

5 Tie cord or lacing around drum, and tie ends together to make a loop for hanging ornament. Glue holly sprig to drum at knot.

6 Cut off pointed ends of two round toothpicks; dip one end of each in glue, and insert into beads to make drumsticks. Glue drumsticks to drum.

7 Apply a light coat of acrylic sealer for protective finish. If desired, personalize ornament, using permanent marking pen.

MORE IDEAS FOR ORNAMENTS

Bundles of cinnamon sticks, *glued together and tied with ribbon, make quick, fragrant ornaments. Embellish the ribbon with a sprig of greenery.*

Miniature dried rosebuds *make delicate ornaments. Secure the rosebuds to a 2" (5 cm) Styrofoam® ball, following the instructions for a rosebud topiary on page 91; leave space for pinning and gluing a ribbon hanger in place.*

Paper twist and raffia *make quick country ornaments. Wrap a 10" (25.5 cm) length of untwisted paper twist around a 2" (5 cm) Styrofoam ball, securing it with several pieces of raffia. Also secure raffia for the hanger, using hot glue.*

Simple designs, *applied with paint pens, can add extra sparkle to glass ornaments. Replace the wire hangers with bows of gold cording and ribbon.*

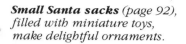
Small Santa sacks (page 92), filled with miniature toys, make delightful ornaments.

Bundles of twigs, tied with jute or ribbon, make simple, rustic ornaments. Embellish the ornament with greenery and a small bird; then spray it with an acrylic sealer.

Cinnamon sticks and clothespins, painted like Santas, are fun for all ages. Use nontoxic acrylic paints for the simple Santa faces; secure strings for hangers, using a drop of hot glue.

Clear plastic balls that snap together can be filled with cherished mementos to make special keepsake ornaments.

TRIMMING THE TREE

Trimmings, such as garlands and bows, are available in an endless variety. These finishing touches unify the tree, even when several styles of ornaments are used together. Choose items that are in keeping with the color scheme and theme of the tree. Some trimmings work better for Victorian decorating styles, while others may be either whimsical, glitzy, or rustic.

Ribbon is wrapped loosely around the tree, spiraling from top to bottom.

Bows (page 74) secured to branches with wire unify a tree with color and repetition.

Purchased trims, such as the ruched paper trim shown here, can be strewn on branches as garlands.

Ornaments *clustered in groups of three have more impact than single ornaments.*

    Streamers *are made by wiring five strands of ribbon together, looping them at one end. Attach the wire to the top of the tree, letting the streamers fall freely, or tuck them lightly into the branches. The dried fruits may either be purchased or made, using a food dehydrator.*

Tassels *hung on the tips of branches have the look of traditional elegance.*

Bridal illusion, *English netting, or other types of net can be tucked between branches to fill in any bare areas.*

Tree skirts can be fast and easy to sew. An unlined tree skirt (opposite), made from prequilted fabric, is especially quick to make. A pregathered ruffle trim is a simple way to add detailing to the edge of the unlined skirt. Or for a wider ruffle with more fullness, you can make your own from coordinating fabric.

Lined tree skirts (right) are made using a stitch-and-turn method. Low-loft batting adds body to the tree skirt, and optional welting defines the outer edge. A ruffle may be added to the outer edge instead of welting, if desired.

For extra embellishment, appliqués can be added to either of these tree skirts.

Holiday wreath appliqués (page 44) *trim the unlined tree skirt, opposite. The wreaths are a variation of the traditional Dresden Plate quilt design.*

Heart appliqués (page 38) *embellish this lined tree skirt. The hearts may be used as pockets to hold sprigs of greenery, candy, or small gifts.*

HOW TO SEW AN UNLINED TREE SKIRT

MATERIALS

- 1¼ yd. (1.15 m) prequilted fabric.
- 1½ yd. (1.4 m) single-fold bias tape, to match the prequilted fabric.
- 1⅛ yd. (1.05 m) fabric for 2" (5 cm) ruffle, 2 yd. (1.85 m) fabric for 3" to 4" (7.5 to 10 cm) ruffle, or 4 yd. (3.7 m) pregathered ruffle trim.

CUTTING DIRECTIONS

Cut prequilted fabric as in steps 1 to 3, below. If you are making your own ruffle, cut eight fabric strips, across the width of the fabric, two times the desired finished width of the ruffle plus 1" (2.5 cm) for seam allowances.

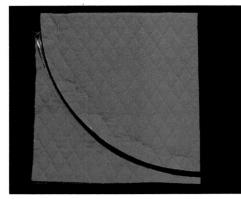

1 Fold 1¼ yd. (1.15 m) of fabric in half lengthwise, then crosswise. Using a straightedge and pencil, mark an arc on fabric, measuring 21" to 22" (53.5 to 56 cm) from folded center of fabric. Cut on marked line through all layers.

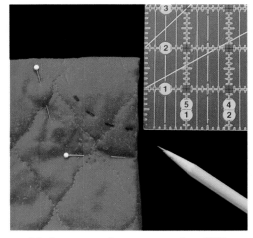

2 Mark a second arc, measuring 1¾" (4.5 cm) from folded center of fabric. Cut on marked line.

3 Cut along one folded edge; this will be the center back of tree skirt.

(Continued)

4 Pin bias tape to back edges and center opening of tree skirt, with right sides together and raw edges matching; stitch along the first foldline of the bias tape. Clip seam allowances around the center circle; trim corners.

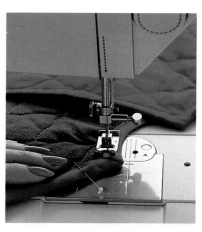

5 Press bias tape to wrong side of skirt; pin in place, mitering tape at corners. Stitch close to folded edge. If pregathered ruffle trim is used, omit steps 6 to 8.

6 Stitch short ends of fabric strips for ruffle together in ¼" (6 mm) seams, right sides together. Fold pieced strip in half lengthwise, right sides together; stitch across ends in ¼" (6 mm) seam. Turn right side out, and press.

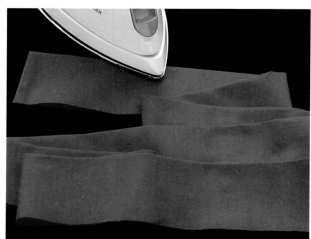

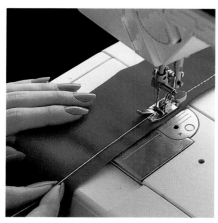

7 Zigzag over a cord a scant ½" (1.3 cm) from raw edges of ruffle.

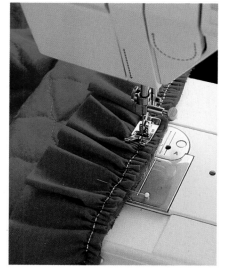

8 Divide ruffle strip and curved outer edge of tree skirt into eighths; pin-mark. Place strip on curved edge, right sides together, matching raw edges and pin marks; pull cord, gathering ruffle to fit.

9 Stitch ruffle to lower edge of skirt, right sides together. If pregathered ruffle trim is used, fold over ends of ruffle ½" (1.3 cm) at back edges of skirt.

10 Turn seam allowances to wrong side of skirt; topstitch the ruffle in place, stitching through all layers. Apply the holiday wreath appliqués (page 44) or heart appliqués (page 38), if desired.

MATERIALS

- 1¼ yd. (1.15 m) face fabric.
- 1¼ yd. (1.15 m) lining fabric.
- 45" (115 cm) square low-loft quilt batting.
- 4 yd. (3.7 m) purchased welting; ruffle trim may be used instead of welting, as for unlined tree skirt.

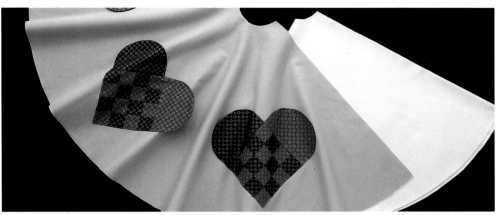

1 Cut face fabric as on page 35, steps 1 to 3; cut the lining, using face fabric as pattern. Make and apply heart appliqués (page 38) or holiday wreath appliqués (page 44) to tree skirt, if desired.

2 Stitch welting, if desired, to curved outer edge on right side of lining, using a zipper foot and matching raw edges; ease welting to fabric as you sew. Curve end of welting into seam allowance at center back.

3 Place the face fabric and the lining right sides together, matching raw edges. Place fabrics on batting, lining side up; pin or baste layers together.

4 Stitch ¼" (6 mm) seam around all edges, leaving 8" (20.5 cm) opening on one straight edge. If the tree skirt has welting, use a zipper foot and stitch just inside the previous stitches, crowding stitches against the welting. Cut batting to the same size as fabric. Clip seam allowances around center circle; trim corners diagonally.

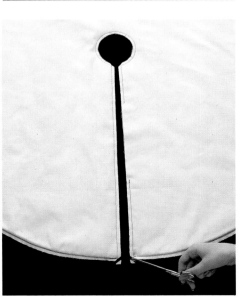

5 Turn fabric right side out; stitch opening closed. Lightly press edges, taking care not to flatten batting. Restitch around appliqués through all layers.

HOW TO MAKE & APPLY HEART APPLIQUÉS

MATERIALS (for five hearts)

- ⅓ yd. (0.32 m) each, red and green printed fabrics, 45" (115 cm) wide.
- ⅔ yd. (0.63 m) lining fabric, 45" (115 cm) wide.
- Embellishments, such as sleigh bells and pinecones.

CUTTING DIRECTIONS

Cut two 2" (5 cm) strips across the width of each fabric. For the top of each heart, cut one green and one red piece, using the heart appliqué pattern on page 125.

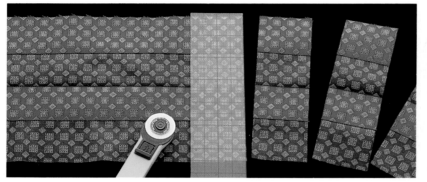 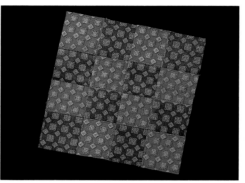

1 Stitch four fabric strips together lengthwise, stitching ¼" (6 mm) seams and alternating colors. Press seam allowances in one direction. Cut 2" (5 cm) strips across pieced strip.

2 Stitch the pieced strips together into five checkerboards, each 6½" (16.3 cm) square, stitching ¼" (6 mm) seams.

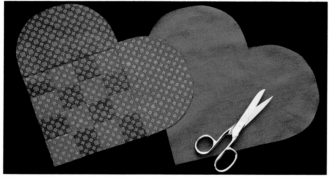 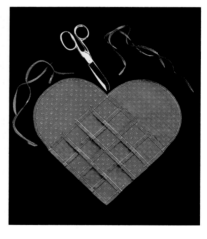

3 Stitch one red and one green heart top to each square, stitching ¼" (6 mm) seams. Cut five hearts from lining fabric, using pieced heart as a guide.

4 Place pieced heart and lining right sides together; pin. Stitch around the edges, stitching ¼" (6 mm) seams and leaving a 2" (5 cm) opening on one side of the checkboard. Trim seam allowances on curves; clip inner corner. Turn heart right side out; press.

5 Arrange hearts on the tree skirt; pin. Edgestitch the sides of hearts in place, starting and ending 1" (2.5 cm) above the checkerboard. Edgestitch inner corner in place for 1" (2.5 cm) on each side.

6 Stitch or glue the desired embellishments at the inner corners of hearts on completed tree skirt. Fill heart pockets with small gifts, candy canes, or pine sprigs.

MORE
IDEAS FOR
TREE SKIRTS

Crazy quilting made from scraps of wool, corduroy, and velveteen adds an old-fashioned appeal to this lined tree skirt (page 37). Quilt the fabric for the tree skirt as on page 81, steps 1 to 3.

Twisted decorative welting defines the edge of this gold lamé lined tree skirt (page 37) for a rich, elegant look.

Radiating trims are stitched on this lined tree skirt (page 37) for an old-world look. The trims are applied to the face fabric before the lining is stitched.

Wide ruffling on this unlined tree skirt (page 35) is bunched and tied with satin bows. The prequilted fabric, eyelet ruffles, and bows are all in ivory to unify the design.

The Holiday Table

a

b

c

Enhance holiday table settings with table runners for the dining table as well as for side tables and buffets.

The holiday wreath table runner **(a)** features the traditional Dresden Plate quilt block, modified to make a wreath with a bow. For easy appliqués, the wedge-shaped pieces for the wreath are stitched together with ¼" (6 mm) seams, and the wreath is appliquéd to the project as one circular piece. The wedge pattern (page 124) includes the necessary seam allowances. For the bow loops and knots, fabric pieces are pressed over cardboard templates, ensuring that the shapes are pressed accurately. Seam allowances are not included in the template patterns; add ¼" (6 mm) when cutting the fabric for the loops and knots. This table runner has five quilt blocks and measures 16" × 70" (40.5 × 178 cm). Matching placemats are on page 51.

Two other styles for table runners include a table runner with a mitered hem **(b)** and another with a contrasting mitered band **(c)**. Both of these styles are unquilted and are variations of the placemats with mitered hems and mitered bands on page 48. These table runners may be custom-made to any size. The yardages required and cutting directions are based on the desired finished size.

HOW TO SEW A HOLIDAY WREATH TABLE RUNNER

MATERIALS

- ⅞ yd. (0.8 m) background fabric.
- 1 yd. (0.95 m) fabric for sashing, borders, and binding.
- 1¼ yd. (1.05 m) backing fabric.
- Low-loft quilt batting.
- Materials for wreath appliqués, listed on page 44.

CUTTING DIRECTIONS

Cut five 13" (33 cm) squares from background fabric. Cut one 20" × 74" (51 × 188 cm) rectangle each from quilt batting and backing fabric, piecing the backing fabric. Cut one 1½" (3.8 cm) strip and ten 2½" (6.5 cm) strips, to be used for sashing, borders, and binding, cutting the strips across the width of the fabric. From the 1½" (3.8 cm) strip, cut three pieces, each 13" (33 cm) long. From one of the 2½" (6.5 cm) strips, cut two pieces, each 13" (33 cm) long; from the remainder of this strip, cut a piece 1½" × 13" (3.8 × 33 cm). Cut five wreath appliqués as on page 44.

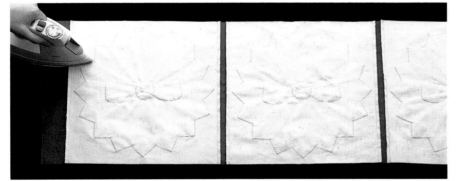

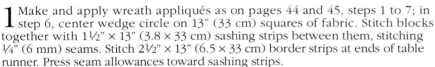

1 Make and apply wreath appliqués as on pages 44 and 45, steps 1 to 7; in step 6, center wedge circle on 13" (33 cm) squares of fabric. Stitch blocks together with 1½" × 13" (3.8 × 33 cm) sashing strips between them, stitching ¼" (6 mm) seams. Stitch 2½" × 13" (6.5 × 33 cm) border strips at ends of table runner. Press seam allowances toward sashing strips.

2 Measure length of pieced block strip down the middle. Cut two border strips to this measurement from 2½" (6.5 cm) strips; piece strips as necessary.

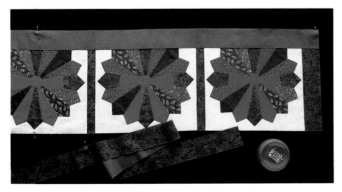

3 Mark centers of border strips and pieced block strip. Pin one border strip along edge of block strip, right sides together, matching ends and center. Stitch; press seam allowances toward border strip. Repeat for other side.

4 Place backing fabric right side down; place batting over backing fabric. Place pieced block strip, right side up, over batting; baste layers together. Trim backing and batting even with raw edges of pieced block strip.

(Continued)

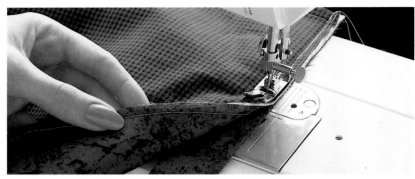

5 Piece remaining 2½" (6.5 cm) strips together as necessary for four binding strips. Press binding strips in half lengthwise, wrong sides together. Place binding strip for one long edge of table runner on pieced block strip, matching raw edges; stitch binding ¼" (6 mm) from raw edges. Trim ends of binding strip even with ends of runner.

6 Wrap binding strip around the edge, covering stitching line on backing side; pin. Stitch in the ditch from the right side, catching binding strip on backing side.

7 Stitch binding strip on remaining long edge as in steps 5 and 6. Stitch binding strips on short ends as in step 5, leaving ends of binding extending ½" (1.3 cm) beyond finished edges; secure binding as in step 6, folding ends over finished edges.

8 Quilt table runner by stitching around appliqués and border, using monofilament nylon thread in needle, and thread to match backing fabric in bobbin. (Contrasting thread was used to show detail.)

HOW TO SEW A HOLIDAY WREATH APPLIQUÉ

MATERIALS (for five or six appliqués)

- Scraps of fabrics in desired prints or solid colors.
- ¼ yd. (0.25 m) fabric for bow of wreath, in a dominant color.
- Small bowl of spray starch.
- Cardboard, for templates.
- Monofilament nylon thread.

CUTTING DIRECTIONS

Transfer bow loop and bow knot templates (page 124) onto cardboard; cut. Using templates, cut one knot and two loops for each block, adding ¼" (6 mm) seam allowances when cutting; turn loop template over for second loop. Transfer wedge pattern (page 124) onto paper. Cut two wedges from bow fabric and fourteen wedges from fabric scraps in desired prints or solid colors for each appliqué; seam allowances are included on wedge pattern.

1 Add lace overlays to some of the fabrics, if desired, by placing right side of wedge face down on wrong side of lace; machine-baste scant ¼" (6 mm) from edges. Trim lace to size of wedge.

2 Fold wide end of one wedge in half, right sides together; stitch ¼" (6 mm) seam across end. Turn right side out, forming point. Press wedge, with seam centered on wrong side of wedge. On light-colored and lightweight fabrics, trim excess fabric from back of the wedge, leaving ¼" (6 mm) seam allowances. Repeat for remaining wedges.

3 Arrange wedges in a circle, with wedges for tails of bow (arrows) separated by one wedge.

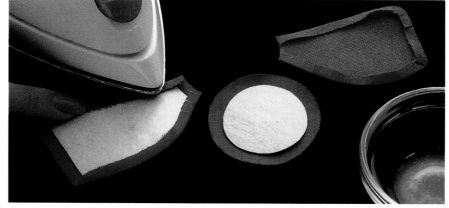

4 Stitch two wedges together, right sides together, stitching ¼" (6 mm) seam along adjoining side. Continue to stitch wedges together until circle is completed. Press seams to one side. Repeat steps for remaining holiday wreath appliqués.

5 Center bow loop and bow knot templates on wrong side of fabric pieces. Spray starch into small bowl; dab starch on section of seam allowance. Using tip of dry iron, press seam allowance over edge of template. Continue around appliqués, except do not press under small ends of bow loops. Remove templates. Repeat for the remaining knot and loop pieces. Press all the pieces right side up.

6 Arrange wreaths on right side of fabric; pin in place. Blindstitch around outer edge, using monofilament nylon thread in the needle; stitch as close to edge as possible, just catching appliqué with widest swing of blindstitch. (Contrasting thread was used to show detail.)

7 Pin or glue-baste bows and knots in place on wreaths; blindstitch in place, as in step 6.

HOLIDAY PLACEMATS

Placemats can be made in a variety of styles for any holiday table setting, from formal to casual. They can be used alone or coordinated with table runners (page 42). Made from fine linens, a placemat with a mitered hem **(a)** is a simple yet elegant style for formal dining. The placemat with a contrasting mitered band **(b)** is a bordered variation of this style. The braid-trimmed placemat **(c)** uses lavish trims for another elegant style.

For more casual table settings, the package placemat **(d)**, ribbon-trimmed at the corners, is both practical and fun. The quilt-as-you-go placemat **(e)**, made with a quick piecing and quilting method, is also embellished at the corners. The holiday wreath placemat **(f)**, another quilted style, uses a wreath variation of the traditional Dresden Plate quilt design.

HOW TO SEW A PLACEMAT WITH A MITERED HEM

MATERIALS (for six placemats)

• Fabric, yardage depending on size of project; for size given below, you will need 1½ yd. (1.4 m).

CUTTING DIRECTIONS

Determine the desired finished size. To this measurement, add twice the desired depth of the hem plus ½" (1.3 cm) for turning under the edges. A good finished size for a placemat suitable for a formal table setting is 14" × 18½" (35.5 × 47.3 cm) with a 1¼" (3.2 cm) hem; cut the fabric 17" × 21½" (43 × 54.8 cm).

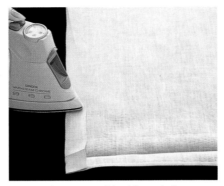

1 Stitch a scant ¼" (6 mm) from edges of fabric. Fold the edges to wrong side; press just beyond the stitching line. Press under desired hem depth on each side of fabric.

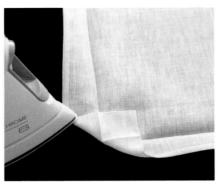

2 Open out corner; fold diagonally so pressed folds match. Press diagonal fold.

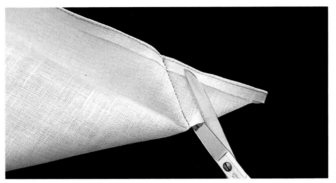

3 Open out corner. Fold through center of corner, right sides together. Stitch on diagonal foldline from step 2. Trim fabric from corner to ¼" (6 mm) from stitching. Press seam open.

4 Press the hem in place, turning corners right side out. Stitch hem, pivoting at corners; use decorative thread, such as rayon or metallic thread, if desired.

HOW TO SEW A PLACEMAT WITH A MITERED BAND

MATERIALS (for six placemats)

• Fabric for contrasting insert, yardage depending on size of project; for size given above, you will need 1¼ yd. (1.15 m).

• Fabric for mitered band, yardage depending on size of project; for size given above, you will need 1½ yd. (1.4 m).

• Fusible interfacing.

CUTTING DIRECTIONS

For each placemat, cut one rectangle from insert fabric equal to the desired *finished* size of the placemat. Cut the fabric for mitered band as for a placemat with mitered hem, above.

1 Follow steps 1 to 3, above. Press band in place, turning corners right side out. Fuse interfacing to wrong side of insert fabric. Place insert on mitered placemat, tucking edges under mitered band; pin.

2 Stitch around the band, securing insert; pivot at corners.

HOW TO SEW A BRAID-TRIMMED PLACEMAT

MATERIALS (for six placemats)

- 2¼ yd. (2.1 m) fabric.
- 2¼ yd. (2.1 m) fusible interfacing.
- 4½ yd. (4.15 m) braid trim.
- Liquid fray preventer, optional.

CUTTING DIRECTIONS

For each placemat, cut two 13" × 19" (33 × 48.5 cm) rectangles from fabric and one from fusible interfacing. Cut two 13" (33 cm) lengths of braid trim; if the trim ravels easily, seal the raw edges with liquid fray preventer.

1 Fuse interfacing to the wrong side of placemat top. Position braid trim as desired at sides; pin in place, and edgestitch.

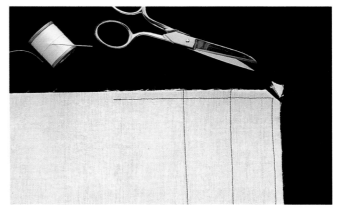

2 Pin placemat pieces right sides together. Stitch around placemat, ¼" (6 mm) from raw edges; leave 4" (10 cm) opening for turning. Trim corners. Turn right side out; press. Slipstitch opening closed.

HOW TO SEW A PACKAGE PLACEMAT

MATERIALS (for six placemats)

- 2¼ yd. (2.1 m) fabric.
- 2¼ yd. (2.1 m) fusible interfacing.
- 7½ yd. (6.9 m) ribbon, about 1" (2.5 cm) wide.
- Liquid fray preventer, optional.

CUTTING DIRECTIONS

For each placemat, cut two 13" × 19" (33 × 48.5 cm) rectangles from fabric and one from fusible interfacing. Cut ribbon into two 10" (25.5 cm) lengths and one 25" (63.5 cm) length.

1 Fuse interfacing to wrong side of placemat top. Pin 10" (25.5 cm) lengths of ribbon across opposite corners of placemat top, keeping ribbon in relaxed position; baste ends in place a scant ¼" (6 mm) from raw edges of placemat top. Trim excess ribbon even with raw edges.

2 Pin placemat pieces right sides together. Stitch around placemat, ¼" (6 mm) from raw edges; leave 4" (10 cm) opening for turning. Trim corners. Turn right side out; press. Slipstitch opening closed. Using 25" (63.5 cm) length of ribbon, tie bow around ribbon at upper corner. Trim ends of ribbon; seal with liquid fray preventer.

HOW TO SEW A QUILT-AS-YOU-GO PLACEMAT

MATERIALS (for six placemats)

- 1¼ yd. (1.5 m) solid-color fabric for background.
- 1¼ yd. (1.5 m) backing fabric.
- Scraps of solid-color and printed fabrics.
- ⅞ yd. (0.8 m) fabric for binding.
- Low-loft quilt batting.

CUTTING DIRECTIONS

Cut six 12½" × 18½" (31.8 × 47.3 cm) rectangles from background fabric. Cut six 13½" × 19½" (34.3 × 49.8 cm) rectangles from the backing fabric and batting.

Cut 1½" (3.8 cm) strips and twelve 3" (7.5 cm) squares from the fabric scraps; cut the squares diagonally to make triangles for corners.

Cut 2½" (6.5 cm) strips from fabric for binding, cutting the strips across the width of the fabric.

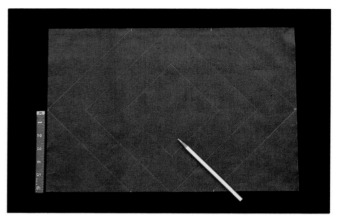

1 Mark right side of background fabric, 6¼" (15.7 cm) from corners, using chalk. Mark diagonal lines across corners, connecting marks. Mark a second set of lines 2" (5 cm) inside marked lines. Mark a square 2" (5 cm) inside second set of lines.

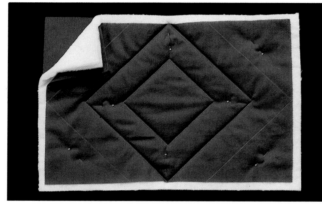

2 Place batting on wrong side of backing fabric; center background fabric on batting, right side up. Pin layers together; quilt the placemat by stitching along the two inside squares.

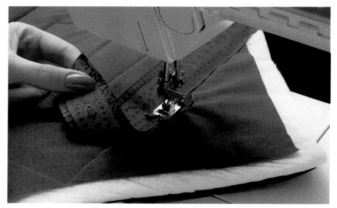

3 Place a fabric strip on background fabric, right sides together, with one raw edge extending ¼" (6 mm) to the outside of marked line. Stitch through all layers, ¼" (6 mm) from raw edge; stitching will be on marked line.

4 Fold strip right side up; finger-press, and pin in place. Place second strip over first, with right sides together and raw edges even.

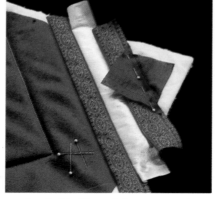

5 Stitch ¼" (6 mm) from raw edges of strips. Fold second strip right side up; finger-press, and pin in place. Repeat for the third strip and for the corner triangle.

6 Trim backing fabric and batting to size of pieced top, trimming ends of strips. Apply binding as on page 44, steps 5 to 7, using four binding strips for each placemat.

HOW TO SEW A HOLIDAY WREATH PLACEMAT

MATERIALS (for six placemats)

- 7/8 yd. (0.8 m) background fabric.
- 1/2 yd. (0.5 m) border fabric.
- 1 1/4 yd. (1.15 m) backing fabric.
- Low-loft quilt batting.
- Materials for wreath appliqués, listed on page 44.

CUTTING DIRECTIONS

For each placemat, cut one 13" (33 cm) square from background fabric, two 3½" × 13" (9 × 33 cm) strips from border fabric, one 13" × 19" (33 × 48.5 cm) rectangle from backing fabric, and one 15" × 21" (38 × 53.5 cm) rectangle from batting. Cut one wreath appliqué, following the cutting directions on page 44.

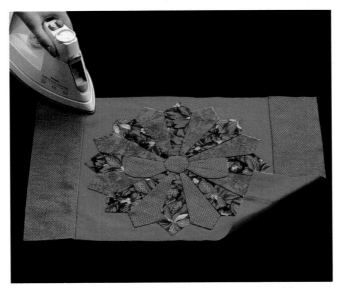

1 Make and apply wreath appliqués as on page 44, steps 1 to 7; in step 6, center wedge circle on 13" (33 cm) square of fabric. Stitch border strips to sides of appliquéd block, stitching ¼" (6 mm) seams; press seam allowances toward border strips.

2 Place backing and placemat top right sides together. Place fabrics on batting, backing side up; pin or baste layers together.

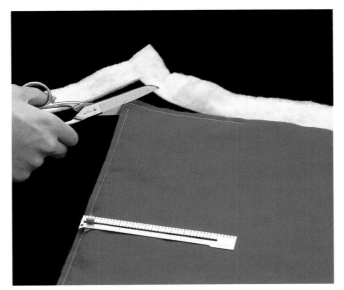

3 Stitch around placemat, ¼" (6 mm) from raw edges of placemat top; leave 4" (10 cm) opening for turning. Trim batting to ⅛" (3 mm); trim corners.

4 Turn placemat right side out; press. Slipstitch opening closed. Quilt placemat by stitching around appliqué and along border strips, using monofilament nylon thread in needle and thread that matches backing fabric in bobbin. (Contrasting thread was used to show detail.)

PAINTED
TABLE LINENS

Tablecloths, placemats, table runners, and napkins provide a simple backdrop for hand-painted embellishments. Select purchased table linens, or sew your own linens, following the instructions for placemats with mitered hems on page 48; by varying the size, these instructions can be used for tablecloths, table runners, and napkins as well as for placemats.

Trace designs from stencils, adapt artwork from greeting cards or pictorial books, or paint original designs. For a unified table, coordinate the painted designs with your china, or create a design to enhance a centerpiece.

Practice the painting techniques on fabric scraps or paper before painting the linens. When painting, protect the work surface by covering it with plastic. Heat-set the paints according to the manufacturer's instructions, and when laundering the linens, use the care method recommended for the fabric.

MATERIALS

- Purchased tablecloth, placemats, table runner, or napkins; or fabric for table linens with mitered hems (page 48).

- Textile paints, including metallic paints, if desired.

- Artist's brushes.

- Pictorial design book or stencils, if desired.

Dilute paint that will be used for a spattered effect. Wet brush with paint, and tap the brush to spatter the paint.

Use stencils for marking designs, if desired. Apply paint to small design areas, using artist's brushes.

Use artwork in pictorial books for design ideas like this geometric design. Mark lines on fabric, using pencil or permanent-ink pen and straightedge.

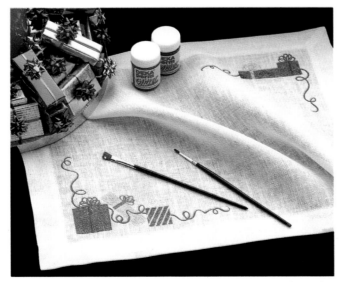

Customize a design to coordinate a tablecloth or placemat with a holiday centerpiece.

Adapt a design from holiday dinnerware by painting a coordinating tablecloth or placemat.

GIFT BOX CENTERPIECES

HOW TO MAKE A GIFT BOX CENTERPIECE

Miniature gift boxes, stacked and mounted on a circular base, create this candle-ring centerpiece.

For best results, select wrapping papers in solid colors or tiny patterns. Purchase the miniature bows at craft stores. Or make them with a bow maker, available at stores specializing in miniatures.

MATERIALS

- Foam board, ⅜" (1 cm) thick.
- Styrofoam® board, ⅜" (1 cm) thick; 18 match boxes can be substituted for part of the ⅜" (1 cm) Styrofoam.
- Styrofoam board, 1" (2.5 cm) thick; 27 snack-size candy boxes can be substituted.
- Assorted wrapping papers.

- 45 miniature bows.
- 1½-yd. (1.4 m) length of ribbon, ⅜" (1 cm) wide.
- Wax adhesive, such as Mini-Hold©.
- Mat knife; cellophane tape; craft glue; hot glue gun and glue sticks.
- One 4" (10 cm) candle or three tapered candles.

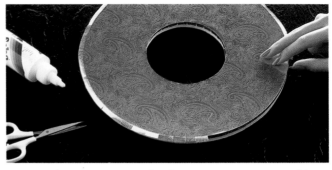

1 Draw a circle with 5½" (14 cm) radius on foam board, using compass. Keeping compass at same center point, draw another circle with radius of 2⅛" (5.3 cm). Cut on marked lines, using mat knife, to make centerpiece base.

2 Trace base on wrong side of wrapping paper; cut, adding ¼" (6 mm) at inner and outer edges. Glue in place to top and sides of base, slashing as necessary.

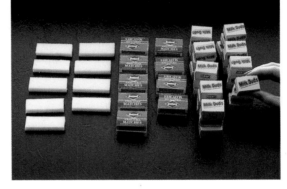

3 Cover edges of base with ribbon, securing it with craft glue.

4 Cut 9 rectangles from ⅜" (1 cm) Styrofoam board, each measuring 1" × 2¾" (2.5 × 7 cm). Use 18 match boxes and 27 snack-size candy boxes for remaining boxes; or cut 18 rectangles from ⅜" (1 cm) Styrofoam, each 1½" × 2½" (3.8 × 6.5 cm), and 27 rectangles from 1" (2.5 cm) Styrofoam, each 1" × 1½" (2.5 × 3.8 cm).

5 Wrap boxes in assorted papers. Attach bows, using hot glue, to all 1" × 2¾" (2.5 × 7 cm) wrapped boxes and to 9 of the wrapped match boxes. Attach bows to wrapped candy boxes, placing 18 on box ends and 9 on box sides.

6 Arrange boxes without bows on base, placing short sides of boxes at inside of base; secure temporarily with wax; once positioned, secure with hot glue.

7 Arrange 2 candy boxes and 1 match box on top of match boxes from step 6; place inside candy box on end, middle candy box on its side, and the match box in front. Secure with wax.

8 Place remaining candy boxes as shown, positioning each box on its side; secure with wax. Adjust as necessary, so boxes are evenly spaced. Secure with hot glue.

9 Stack 1" × 2¾" (2.5 × 7 cm) boxes on candy boxes, as shown; secure with hot glue. Place candle in the center of the ring.

MORE IDEAS FOR CENTERPIECES

Wreath, *propped against the wall, provides a centerpiece for a side table and does not interfere with serving space. Position a cluster bow (page 74) at the top of the wreath, and add long streamers to flow onto the table.*

Tinsel-filled ornaments *(page 23), clustered in a bowl and surrounded with greens, make a simple centerpiece. The ornaments are set aglow with miniature battery-operated lights.*

Fresh evergreen sprays, *placed end-to-end and topped with a bow, make a quick and attractive centerpiece. Candles are nestled in the greens.*

Artificial garland, *arranged in an S shape and embellished with golden artichokes and gilded pinecones and pomegranates, creates an easy and elegant centerpiece. This style is especially suited for long tables.*

HOW TO MAKE A FRESH EVERGREEN SPRAY CENTERPIECE

MATERIALS

- Fresh tips from various evergreens; cedar greens work well for the base.
- 22-gauge or 24-gauge wire; wire cutter; floral tape.
- Embellishments as desired, such as candles, ribbon, and berries.

1 Layer fresh greens, and secure stems with wire. Wrap wired stems with floral tape to protect the table, stretching the tape as it is applied. Repeat to make two garlands.

2 Overlap and wire stems of layered greens together; cover with floral tape.

3 Make bow with long streamers (page 74), and secure to greens, concealing wired stems. Twist and loop the streamers among the greens. Arrange candles and other embellishments as desired.

HOW TO MAKE AN ARTIFICIAL GARLAND CENTERPIECE

MATERIALS

- Artificial garland, 18" to 24" (46 to 61 cm) longer than desired length of centerpiece.
- French ribbon, about 18" (46 cm) longer than garland.
- Artichokes; dried pomegranates; pinecones; cinnamon sticks.
- Gold aerosol paint; gold wax-based paint.
- 26-gauge wire; wire cutter; floral tape.

1 Arrange garland in S shape on the table; adjust length, if necessary. Twist ribbon loosely throughout garland.

2 Apply gold aerosol paint to artichokes; spray the pinecones, if desired. Rub gold wax-based paint on pomegranates to add highlights. Wire pinecones and cinnamon sticks as on page 66.

3 Place artichokes near the center of the arrangement. Secure pinecones and cinnamon sticks to garland. Arrange the pomegranates between pinecones and cinnamon sticks. Arrange the candles as desired.

TABLE ACCESSORIES

Small accessories, like napkin rings and etched glassware, add charm to each place setting. Easy to make, these finishing touches make a holiday table festive.

Ornaments, *such as French horns and wreaths, make inexpensive napkin rings that can double as favors for guests.*

Lace napkin rings (opposite) *complement a table setting with a Victorian theme.*

Garland sprig napkin ring *(opposite), embellished with artificial holly, is quick to make.*

Sheer and pleated ribbons, tied around napkins and stemware, add a festive touch.

Etching (below), done using a rub-on etching stencil and etching cream, turns inexpensive glassware into holiday goblets and plates.

HOW TO MAKE TABLE ACCESSORIES

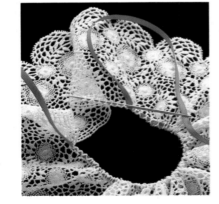

Lace napkin rings. Cut 20" (51 cm) length of flat lace with a heading; stitch short ends together. Using a tapestry needle, weave 32" (81.5 cm) length of ⅛" (3 mm) ribbon through the lace heading. Gather lace around napkin; tie ribbon in a bow.

Garland sprig napkin rings. Cut individual sprigs from an artificial garland. Wrap sprigs around a cylinder, such as cardboard tube, for shape; twist ends of sprigs together. Secure holly with hot glue.

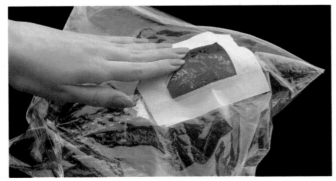

1 **Etched glassware.** Use rub-on etching stencil and etching cream, available from craft stores. Apply a border of masking tape around stencil, overlapping the edges. Cover area of glass that will not be etched with plastic and masking tape.

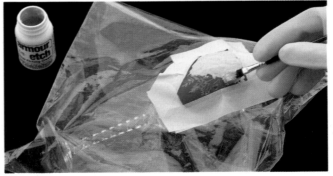

2 Apply a thick layer of etching cream over entire design area, using a soft-bristle brush; allow etching cream to remain on design for 1 minute. Rinse design thoroughly to remove all etching cream; pat area dry. Remove stencil, plastic, and masking tape.

TABLE
ENSEMBLES

Whether you are planning a casual get-together with friends for cookies and hot chocolate, a formal dinner party for coworkers, or a family gathering for Christmas dinner, holiday table settings can have a special flair. For a party that will be remembered, coordinate the table appointments down to the last detail.

Victorian setting *is used for this formal dinner party. Victorian cards (page 117) at each place setting establish the theme; place cards are made to match. Tassels accent the candlesticks, and a fresh evergreen spray centerpiece (page 57) is trimmed with a lavish gold bow. Lace napkin rings (page 59) add to the romantic look.*

Casual Santa theme *is set with Santa sacks (page 92). Filled with tiny gifts, small sacks are favors for the guests, and larger sacks create the centerpiece. Placemats with contrasting mitered bands (page 48) and garland sprig napkin rings (page 59) add to the festive look. Santa cinnamon sticks (page 31), painted at one end, are used for stirring the cider.*

Festive table setting *starts with star-studded china and gold-rimmed glassware. The table linens are painted with metallics to coordinate with the china (page 52), and sheer metallic ribbon makes elegant napkin rings.*

A centerpiece of tinsel-filled ornaments (page 23) is aglow with miniature battery-operated lights. Small presents for the guests in decoupaged gift boxes (page 113) accent each place setting.

Around The
House

Nothing echoes a Christmas tradition more than wreaths. You can make your own from fresh, preserved, or artificial greens. Or purchase ready-made wreaths and add your own embellishments. Fresh evergreen and eucalyptus wreaths, both easy to make, add fragrance to a room. Other wreath styles, including grapevine and twig wreaths, are available at craft and floral stores.

You may choose to embellish an entire wreath, use a third of the wreath as the design area, or add a single embellishment. It is usually more attractive if the focal point of the design is slightly offset.

Choose embellishments that are in scale with the size of the wreath, and vary the size of the embellishments so there will be a dominant focal point, with smaller items that complement it. Choose items that are harmonious in style, yet provide some contrast in color and texture. Several suggestions for embellishing wreaths are shown on pages 66 to 69.

HOW TO MAKE A FRESH EVERGREEN WREATH

MATERIALS

- Fresh greens.
- 22-gauge or 24-gauge paddle floral wire; wire cutter; pruning shears.
- Coat hanger.
- Ribbon and embellishments as desired.

1 Shape coat hanger into circle. Cut greens into sprigs. Wire three sprigs to hanger, with tips facing up, placing two in front and one in back; wrap wire at base of sprigs.

2 Continue wrapping clusters of greens with wire, overlapping each cluster to conceal wire. When coat hanger is covered, cut some full tips of greens and wire them to hanger, concealing ends of sprigs.

HOW TO MAKE A EUCALYPTUS WREATH

MATERIALS

- Ready-made straw wreath.
- Eucalyptus with fine stems; two or three bunches will be sufficient for most wreath sizes.
- 22-gauge or 24-gauge paddle floral wire; wire cutter; pruning shears.
- Ribbon and embellishments as desired.

1 Cut eucalyptus in half or in thirds, so each sprig is 6" to 7" (15 to 18 cm) long. Secure the bottom 1" (2.5 cm) of several sprigs to wreath with wire, wrapping the wire around wreath; cover front and sides of wreath.

2 Continue adding sprigs to front and sides of wreath; layer sprigs and wrap with wire, working in one direction. Stagger the length of the tips randomly.

3 Lift tips of sprigs at starting point, and secure last layer of sprigs under them. Make a wire loop for hanging; secure loop to back of the wreath. Embellish as desired.

TIPS FOR EMBELLISHING WREATHS

Secure ribbon tails with hot glue, arranging twists and loops.

Make picks by grouping items together. Attach wire to items as necessary. Wrap stems and wires with floral tape.

Separate bunches of dried flowers by holding them over steam for 1 to 2 minutes; remove from steam and pull stems apart gently.

Attach wire to pinecone by wrapping wire around bottom layers of pinecone.

Add wire as necessary to fragile stems of dried flowers, to strengthen them. Wrap stem and wire with floral tape.

Attach wire to cinnamon stick by inserting it through the length of the stick; wrap the wire around the stick, twisting ends at middle. Trim wire, leaving 6" (15 cm) ends for attaching to wreath.

Create a base for anchoring embellishments by wiring a piece of floral foam, which has been covered with moss, to the wreath. Attach embellishments to moss-covered base.

Shape an artificial wreath made on a single wire into a candy cane or swag. Cut the wreath apart where the wire was joined.

Add luster to pinecones by applying glossy brown aerosol paint.

Spray artificial snow on wreath for a lightly flocked appearance.

Highlight twigs and vines with frost or glitter aerosol paint.

Keep a balanced look when embellishing an entire wreath by dividing wreath into three or four sections; distribute items evenly within each section.

Display wreath over a length of wide ribbon for added color. Embellish the top of the ribbon with a sprig.

MORE IDEAS FOR WREATHS

Snowman ornaments (page 26) add a whimsical touch to this artificial wreath. The light misting of artificial snow, the tiny purchased sleds, and the candy canes carry out the wintery holiday theme.

Victorian wreath made from eucalyptus (page 65) features a pearlescent cherub on a pastel satin bow. Statice and clustered pastel embellishments are used throughout the wreath.

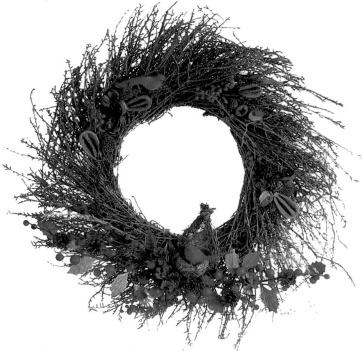

Musical theme on this fresh evergreen wreath (page 65) was created using purchased instrument ornaments and paper fans (page 19) made from sheet music.

Dried naturals are the primary embellishments for this ready-made twig wreath. The bird's nest, slightly off-center on the wreath, becomes the focal point.

Silver and gold *are combined for this wreath. Silver aerosol paint is used to highlight the greens, and a sheer silver ribbon becomes a strong focal point. Touches of gold are introduced in the smaller embellishments.*

Evergreen bouquet *of mixed greens and pinecones is wired asymmetrically onto a ready-made grapevine wreath for a quick embellishment. The narrow French ribbon is wrapped loosely around the wreath.*

Gold and red metallics *are used for a dramatic effect, and the embellishments are offset for even more impact. The ready-made straw wreath used as the base was concealed with metallic ribbon and tiny garland.*

Apples and popcorn *are used as the dominant embellishments for this fresh wreath of mixed greens (page 65). To carry out the natural look, nuts and pinecones are also used.*

GARLANDS

Graceful swags of garland add a dramatic touch to a room. Whether the garlands are made from fresh, preserved, or artificial greens, they can be embellished for an impressive statement.

Fresh garlands are quick and easy to make, and handmade fresh garlands have a fuller shape than purchased ones. When making your own, mix different varieties of greens for added color and texture. Fresh cuttings can often be purchased by weight from nurseries. Cedar greens work especially well for indoor use; they do not shed, and they keep their color longer than most varieties.

For the realistic look of fresh garlands, use dried or preserved greens. They last longer than fresh garlands and can be used for more than one season. For a garland that can be used year after year, use artificial greens. To add the fragrance of evergreen, embellish the garland with scented pinecones or tuck in a few sprigs of fresh greens.

HOW TO MAKE A FRESH GARLAND

MATERIALS

- Fresh greens.
- Lightweight rope or twine.
- 22-gauge paddle floral wire or chenille stems.
- Pruning shears.
- Wire cutter.

2 Continue wiring greens around rope, overlapping them to conceal the wire. At desired length, wire full tips of greens to bottom of garland, concealing ends of sprigs.

1 Tie rope to solid overhead object, such as ceiling-mounted plant hook. Cut fresh greens into sprigs. Wire three sprigs to rope, with tips facing up, placing two in front and one in back; wrap wire at the base of the sprigs.

3 Cut the wire and rope at ends of garland; knot ends, forming loops for hanging, if desired.

MORE IDEAS FOR GARLANDS

Garland *is used traditionally to dress the mantel. To secure the garland without nailing into the mantel itself, cut a 1 × 1 board the length of the mantel. Stain or paint the board to match the mantel, and pound nails into the board for securing the garland.*

Swag *is draped high above a fireplace, and sprays are displayed on each side. To make a pair of sprays from an artificial garland, cut a 9-foot (2.75 meter) garland in half. Fold each piece in half, creating two sprays, and embellish them as desired.*

Safety note: *Do not leave any open flame, including candles, unattended. For fireplaces, always use a fire screen. (Screen was removed for photo effect.)*

Bow-shaped garland is hung over the fireplace instead of a wreath. Tie a wide ribbon to the ends of the garland, and hang the garland from the ribbon.

Fresh garland is used to decorate a bannister. To protect wood surfaces, use chenille stems instead of wire when making the garland.

HOLIDAY BOWS

Lavish bows and streamers are often a finishing touch for holiday decorations. Use ribbons in the traditional red and green, or in colors to match the decor of the room.

The key to achieving a luxurious look is to be generous with the ribbon. The size of the bow should be in proportion to the project being embellished. For example, large garlands require large, full bows with long streamers; for large bows, use wide, stiff ribbons.

Craft ribbon is available in several fabric types, including taffeta, moiré, satin, and velvet. French ribbon, sometimes called wired ribbon, makes beautiful bows. The fine wires that run along the edges of the ribbon can be bent into curves and folds, giving bows an old-world look that is distinctly elegant. For a more homespun or country look, bows can be made from paper twist.

Two styles of bows are so versatile that they meet most holiday decorating needs: the cluster bow and the traditional bow.

The cluster bow can easily be made in any size. To estimate the ribbon yardage, multiply the desired diameter of the bow times the number of loops desired. Add 6" (15 cm) to this measurement for the center loop plus the desired amount for tails and extra streamers.

The traditional bow is commonly used for wreaths, but also works well for elegant packages. For a 7" to 8" (18 to 20.5 cm) bow, you will need 2½ yd. (2.3 m) of ribbon.

Plaid taffeta ribbon is used for the large cluster bow on this spray of greens. For added embellishment, pinecones surround the bow.

Two layers of French ribbon, *treated as one, are used for the cluster bow on this tiered plate stand.*

Sheer metallic ribbon *in cluster bows adorns a pair of candlesticks.*

Taffeta French ribbon, *tied into a traditional bow, embellishes this Christmas package.*

Paper twist *is used instead of ribbon for the traditional bow on a fruit basket.*

French ribbon *makes the cluster bow for this ivy plant. For an ivy wreath, secure the vines to a wire wreath base.*

HOW TO MAKE A TRADITIONAL BOW

MATERIALS

- 2½-yd. to 3-yd. (2.3 to 2.75 m) length of ribbon, 2" to 2½" (5 to 6.5 cm) wide.

- 22-gauge or 24-gauge floral wire; or chenille wire for bows that will be wired to packages or around woodwork.

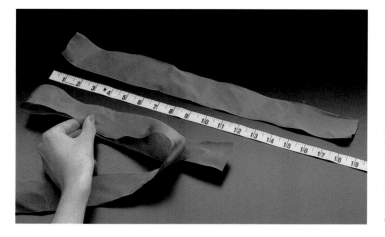

1 Cut 18" (46 cm) length of ribbon; set aside for center tie. Starting 8" to 12" (20.5 to 30.5 cm) from end of remaining length of ribbon, fold 3½" to 4" (9 to 10 cm) loop with right side of ribbon facing out.

2 Fold a loop toward the opposite side, bringing ribbon underneath the tail to keep the right side of the ribbon facing out.

3 Continue wrapping the ribbon, making loops that fan slightly, until there are three or four loops on each side with a second tail extending.

4 Bend wire around ribbon at center; twist wire tightly, gathering ribbon. Hold wire firmly at the top, and turn the bow, twisting wire snug.

5 Fold width of 18" (46 cm) ribbon into thirds through the middle portion of ribbon. Tie ribbon around center of the bow, knotting it on the back of the bow.

6 Separate loops. Trim tails as desired.

HOW TO MAKE A CLUSTER BOW

MATERIALS

- Ribbon in desired width; calculate yardage as on page 74.
- 22-gauge or 24-gauge floral wire; or chenille wire for bows that will be wired to packages or around woodwork.

1 Place thumb and index finger at determined length for tail, with ribbon right side up. Fold the ribbon back on itself at a diagonal, with wrong sides together, so ribbon forms a right angle.

2 Wrap ribbon over thumb to form center loop; secure with fingers. Twist ribbon one-half turn at underside of loop, so the right side of the ribbon faces up.

3 Form first loop. Twist ribbon one-half turn, and form loop on opposite side.

4 Continue forming loops under the previous loops, alternating sides and twisting ribbon so right side always faces up; make each loop slightly larger than the loop above it.

5 When final loop has been formed, insert wire through center of bow. Bend wire around ribbon at center; twist wire tightly, gathering ribbon. Hold wire firmly at the top and turn the bow, twisting wire snug. Separate and shape the loops.

STOCKINGS

Christmas stockings often have sentimental value if they are handmade. They need not be time-consuming projects to be special. Simple stockings can become heirlooms when they are embellished with family keepsakes, such as lace handkerchiefs or sections from tea towels or doilies. Or, use scraps of your favorite fabrics to make a crazy-quilt stocking; these stockings take on special meaning when made from old fabrics or scraps from cherished garments.

For stockings that are dramatic and elegant, select fabrics like velvets, moirés, and tapestries. Or for stockings that look rustic, select corduroys and wools. Pad the stocking with lightweight batting or fleece to add body.

HOW TO SEW A LINED STOCKING

MATERIALS

- ½ yd. (0.5 m) face fabric.
- ½ yd. (0.5 m) lining fabric.
- Low-loft quilt batting or polyester fleece.
- Ribbon, cording, or plastic ring, for hanging stocking.

CUTTING DIRECTIONS

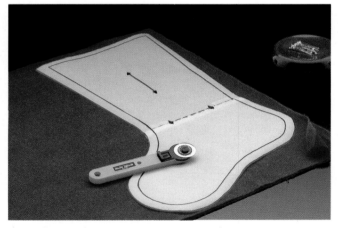

Transfer stocking pattern pieces A and B on pages 122 and 123 to paper. Tape pieces together, matching notches and dotted lines; add ½" (1.3 cm) seam allowances on all sides to make full-size stocking pattern. Cut two stocking pieces, right sides together, from face fabric and two from lining. Also cut two stocking pieces from batting or fleece.

1 Pin lace embellishments, if desired, right side up on right side of stocking front. Trim lace even with raw edges of stocking; baste in place. Baste batting or fleece to wrong side of stocking front and back.

(Continued)

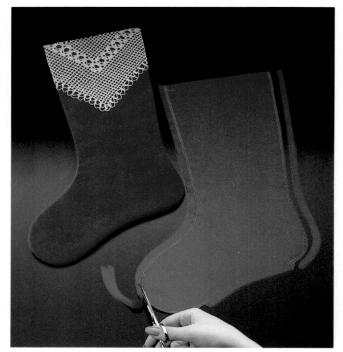

2 Pin the stocking front to the stocking back, right sides together. Stitch ½" (1.3 cm) seam around stocking, leaving top open; stitch again next to first row of stitching, within seam allowances. Trim seam allowances close to stitches. Turn stocking right side out; lightly press.

3 Pin lining pieces, right sides together. Stitch ½" (1.3 cm) seam around lining, leaving top open and bottom unstitched 4" to 6" (10 to 15 cm); stitch again next to first row of stitching, within seam allowances. Trim seam allowances close to stitches.

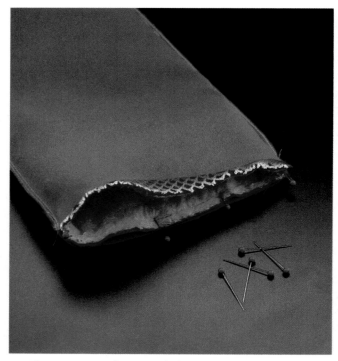

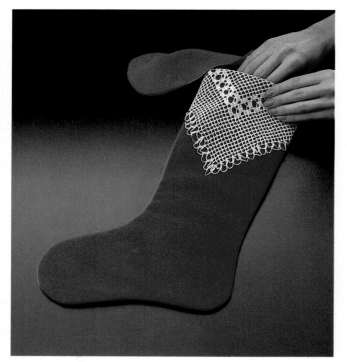

4 Place outer stocking inside lining, right sides together. Pin upper edges, raw edges even; stitch. Turn right side out through opening in lining.

5 Stitch opening closed. Insert lining into the stocking; lightly press upper edge. Handstitch ribbon, cording, or ring at upper edge of stocking for hanger. Edgestitch around upper edge, if desired.

HOW TO SEW A CRAZY-QUILT STOCKING

MATERIALS

- Scraps of fabric for stocking front.
- ⅝ yd. (0.6 m) coordinating fabric for stocking back.
- ⅝ yd. (0.6 m) lining fabric.
- ⅝ yd. (0.6 m) fusible interfacing.
- Low-loft quilt batting or polyester fleece.
- Tear-away stabilizer.

CUTTING DIRECTIONS

Make stocking pattern (page 78), using stocking pattern pieces A and B on pages 122 and 123. Cut two stocking pieces from the lining, right sides together, and two from the batting or fleece. Cut one stocking front from fusible interfacing, with fusible side of interfacing up. Cut fabric scraps into a variety of shapes. Cut one stocking back from coordinating fabric, with right side of fabric down.

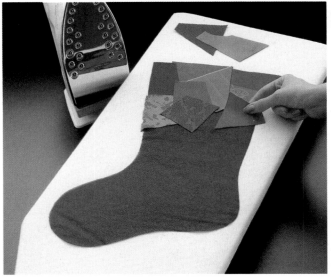

1 Place interfacing piece on ironing board, fusible side up. Arrange fabric scraps, right side up, on interfacing, overlapping edges. Fuse pieces in place.

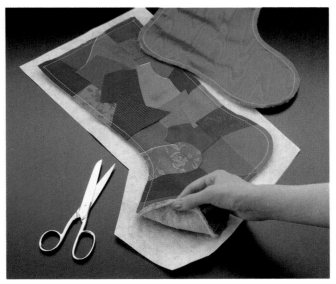

2 Trim fabric edges even with interfacing, from wrong side. Baste batting or fleece to wrong side of stocking front and back pieces; place tear-away stabilizer on batting side of stocking front.

3 Stitch around fabric scraps on stocking front, stitching through all layers with decorative machine stitches, using wide stitches that cover raw edges well. If necessary, trim raw edges of the fabric close to stitches. Remove the tear-away stabilizer.

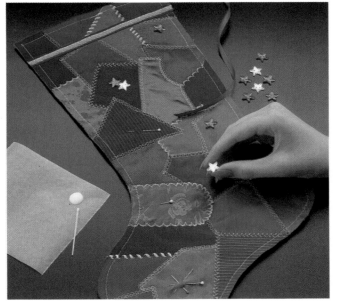

4 Add embellishments, such as ribbons, lace, or buttons, if desired, gluing or stitching them in place. Complete stocking as in steps 2 to 5, opposite.

MORE IDEAS FOR STOCKINGS

Old buttons and lavish streamers turn a simple tapestry stocking into a treasured keepsake.

Beadwork and gold braid elegantly trim this stocking. The trims, hand-stitched in place, create the appearance of a cuff.

Crazy-quilt stocking made from scraps of wool has a rustic appearance. Metallic thread adds sparkle.

Hand-crocheted overlay *creates an heirloom stocking. Cut the overlay from undamaged sections of old table linens.*

Ruffled lace and specialty ribbons *are added to a Christmas stocking for romantic flair.*

Galloon lace *on moiré taffeta makes a distinctive, elegant stocking. Silky ribbons complete the look.*

CONE
TREES

Cone trees are stunning arrangements for buffet tables and side tables. A wide selection of suitable embellishments is available at craft stores and floral shops. Choose from dried naturals, pinecones, fruits, preserved greens, ribbon, and other items, depending on the look you want. Use an inverted basket as a base for the cone tree.

The lemon cone tree (left) may be made with either fresh or artificial lemons. The tree is embellished with gold pinecones, statice, eucalyptus, and cinnamon sticks; a bird perched near the top of the tree adds the finishing touch. To vary the look, apples, pears, or other fruit may be substituted for the lemons.

For a dried-natural cone tree (page 86), make a tree from preserved evergreens, using two types of greens for added depth and texture. Embellish the tree with pinecones, berries, and ribbon, adding statice to give the tree a more delicate look. Artificial greens and berries may be substituted for the natural items.

For either tree, use a Styrofoam® cone as the form, covering it with Spanish moss for the background. The desired embellishments are inserted into the cone using wire or wooden picks, making it easy to rearrange the items until you achieve a balanced look. Add the embellishments, distributing them evenly but not in rows. Work from the bottom of the tree toward the top; trim the pick length as necessary at the top of the tree. Frequently stand back to view the arrangement from all sides. This allows you to check the balance and look for any bare areas that need embellishments.

HOW TO MAKE A LEMON CONE TREE

MATERIALS

- Styrofoam® cone, about 18" (46 cm) high with 5" (12.5 cm) base.
- Woven basket with 5" (12.5 cm) base.
- Spanish moss.
- 18 to 20 small lemons, fresh or artificial.
- Statice and green eucalyptus, about 5 stems of each.
- 10 to 12 cinnamon sticks, 3" (7.5 cm) in length.

- 20 or more pinecones in various sizes; gold metallic aerosol paint.
- Decorative bird, optional.
- 4" (10 cm) wooden floral picks; 3" (7.5 cm) wooden floral picks with wire.
- 18-gauge wire; wire cutter.
- Hot glue gun and glue sticks.

1 Apply hot glue to the top of the inverted basket; secure cone to the basket. Puncture each fresh lemon at stem end with point of 4" (10 cm) wooden pick; insert flat end of pick into punctured lemon for about 2" (5 cm).

2 Secure lemons to the cone by inserting the picks, arranging lemons in a spiral around cone; wrap cone with a string to use as a guide. Arrange the Spanish moss around the lemons, pulling the moss apart so it loosely covers Styrofoam; secure with hot glue.

3 Break the statice into small sprigs ranging from 2" to 6" (5 to 15 cm) long. Insert sprigs into cone, placing longer sprigs at bottom of cone and shorter sprigs toward top. Secure as necessary, using hot glue.

4 Attach a wooden pick with wire to the bottom of each pinecone by wrapping the wire around bottom layers of pinecone. Apply gold paint to the pinecones; for easier application, insert picks into a piece of Styrofoam. When dry, place the pinecones in the arrangement.

5 Attach 18-gauge wire to each cinnamon stick by inserting it through the length of the stick. Wrap the wire around the stick, twisting ends at the middle. Cut off one end of wire, using wire cutter; cut the other end to 2" or 3" (5 to 7.5 cm). Place wired cinnamon sticks in arrangement.

6 Cut eucalyptus into sprigs ranging from 3" to 4" (7.5 to 10 cm) long; break leaves off as necessary to make stem. Insert the sprigs, placing longer pieces at the bottom of the tree. Attach wooden pick to bird; insert near top of arrangement.

HOW TO MAKE A DRIED-NATURAL CONE TREE

MATERIALS

- Styrofoam® cone, about 18" (46 cm) high with 5" (12.5 cm) base.
- Woven basket with 5" (12.5 cm) base.
- Spanish moss.
- Preserved or artificial greens, such as spruce, cedar, and boxwood.
- 20 or more pinecones in various sizes.
- 11 yd. (10.1 m) ribbon, ⅜" (1 cm) wide.
- Several stems of small berries.
- Dried naturals, such as statice or baby's breath.
- 3" (7.5 cm) wooden floral picks with wire.
- Pruning shears; wire cutter.
- Craft glue; hot glue gun and glue sticks.

1 Apply hot glue to the top of the inverted basket; secure cone to basket. Arrange Spanish moss on cone, pulling moss apart so it loosely covers Styrofoam; secure with dots of hot glue, using glue sparingly.

2 Cut greens into sprigs ranging from 3" to 6" (7.5 to 15 cm) long, making angled cuts. Insert the stems into cone, angling the sprigs so they point downward; place longer sprigs at the bottom of the cone and shorter ones toward the top.

3 Cut boxwood into pieces ranging from 3" to 6" (7.5 to 15 cm) long; intersperse other greens with boxwood.

4 Wire pinecones as on page 85, step 4. Insert pinecones, placing larger ones at the bottom and smaller ones at the top.

5 Cut berries into about 20 clusters; wire them to picks, and arrange on cone. Or attach stemmed clusters by inserting stems directly into cone.

6 Cut 15 to 20 clusters of statice; wire them to picks. Insert picks into cone, angling clusters so they point downward.

7 Cut ribbon into 1-yd. (0.95 m) lengths. Fold ribbon, forming three or four loops on each side; leave two tails, with one tail about 2" (5 cm) longer than the other. Attach to a wooden pick with wire, wrapping the wire around the center of the bow several times.

9 Attach bows to cone tree, inserting picks. Attach one bow to the top of the tree; shorten the pick on this bow, if necessary, and secure with glue.

8 Wrap longer tail of bow twice around center, concealing the wire; secure with the remaining wire, and twist wire around pick.

TOPIARY TREES

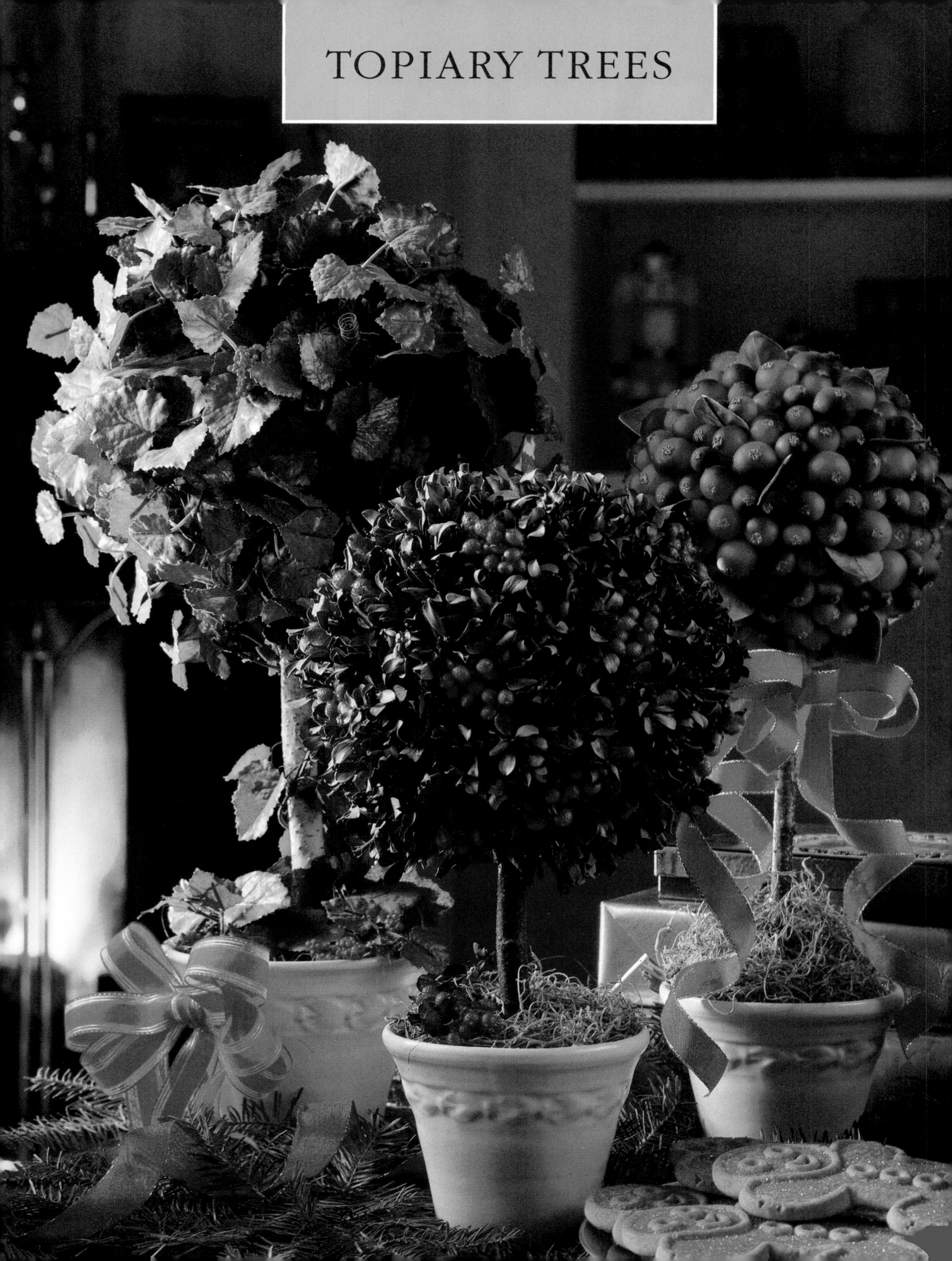

A topiary tree is a classic floral arrangement. The size of topiary trees can be varied, making them suitable for side tables, desks, or end tables. Group several trees of various sizes together for an eye-catching centerpiece on a mantel or buffet table.

For most topiary trees, the base is a Styrofoam® ball secured to a branch or dowel and set into a pot with plaster of Paris. Make the base yourself, following the easy steps below. Or purchase a ready-made base at a floral or craft store; on some purchased bases, the ball is wire mesh instead of Styrofoam. Decorate the topiary with preserved boxwood, grapevine, dried rosebuds, dyed pistachios, or other embellishments, as shown opposite and on the following pages.

HOW TO MAKE A TOPIARY TREE

MATERIALS

- Clay pot or ceramic vase.
- Self-adhesive felt, optional.
- Styrofoam ball.
- Branch or stained dowel for the trunk; additional twigs, if desired.
- Plaster of Paris; disposable container for mixing.
- Heavy-duty aluminum foil.

- Hot glue gun and glue sticks.
- Aerosol paint to match embellishments, if portions of the Styrofoam ball will be exposed between the embellishments.
- Saw, pruning shears, floral wire, and wire cutter may be needed for some projects, depending on materials selected.
- Spanish moss; embellishments as desired.

1 Line clay pot or vase with two layers of aluminum foil. Crumple foil loosely to shape of pot, to allow room for plaster to expand as it dries; edge of foil should be about ¾" (2 cm) below top of pot. If desired, trace bottom of pot or vase onto self-adhesive felt. Cut felt circle, cutting inside marked line; affix to bottom of pot.

2 Apply paint to Styrofoam ball, if desired. Insert trunk of tree into ball to one-half the diameter of ball. Place trunk in pot and adjust height of topiary by cutting trunk to the desired length. Remove the ball from the trunk.

3 Mix plaster of Paris, following the manufacturer's instructions. Pour plaster into the pot, filling pot to edge of foil. When the plaster has started to thicken, insert trunk, making sure it stands straight. Support the trunk, using tape as shown, until plaster has set.

4 Apply hot glue into hole in Styrofoam ball; place ball on trunk. Conceal plaster with Spanish moss or items used to decorate tree. Embellish ball as desired (page 91).

MORE IDEAS
FOR TOPIARY
TREES

Dyed pistachios *are used for casual topiaries that are inexpensive. On one small area at a time, apply hot glue to a painted Styrofoam® ball and quickly secure the pistachios with the unopened end down.*

Tiny dried rosebuds *are delicate and elegant for small topiaries. For easier insertion of the rosebud stems, make holes in the painted Styrofoam ball, using a toothpick, and dip the stems in craft glue before inserting them.*

Flowers and berries *have appealing color and texture. The selections for this topiary tree are hydrangea florets and pepper berries.*

Double topiary trees *are a variation of the basic tree. A ready-made topiary base, purchased at a floral shop, was used for this large floor tree. Pomegranates, oranges, and pinecones, secured with hot glue, are the primary embellishments.*

Sheer French ribbon *coils gently around the topiary tree opposite. Rosebuds and other embellishments are either secured with hot glue or inserted directly into the ball.*

SANTA SACKS

These Santa sacks are made quickly and easily from prestarched fabric. Made in the largest size, they hold almost anything, from poinsettia plants to baked goods. Filled with fingertip towels, medium-size sacks become bathroom accessories. Filled with miniature toys, the smallest sacks make whimsical party favors for the dinner table or ornaments for trees and wreaths. For ease in handling prestarched fabric, place a sheet of wax paper on the work surface and follow the tips on page 28 for shaping the fabric.

HOW TO MAKE A SANTA SACK

MATERIALS

- Prestarched fabric, such as Dip 'n Drape®, Drape 'n Shape, and Fab-U-Drape®.
- Acrylic paint of desired color for sack, in aerosol or liquid form; liquid acrylic paint for contrasting edging; artist's brush.
- Aerosol clear acrylic sealer.
- Cording or leather lacing; sprig of greenery, optional.
- Wax paper; sponge.

CUTTING DIRECTIONS

From prestarched fabric, cut two 15" × 30" (38 × 76 cm) rectangles for the large sack, two 10" × 20" (25.5 × 51 cm) rectangles for the medium sack, or one 5" × 10" (12.5 × 25.5 cm) for the small sack.

1 Large or medium sack. Place the fabric rectangles together; fold over 1" (2.5 cm) on one long edge, and open flat.

2 Dip top layer of fabric quickly into cool water. Lay it back down on the other layer. Smooth layers together, and refold hem for top of sack. Wipe along all edges, using a dampened sponge.

3 Lift fabric at the folded edge, using wet fingers. Form into a cylinder with folded edge facing out. Overlap sides 1" (2.5 cm); press along overlap to close seam.

5 Set sack on wax paper; press inside of sack flat. Stuff crumpled wax paper in the sack, so it holds its shape until dry. Wet fingers, and gather opening of sack slightly; do not overwork fabric. Allow sack to dry thoroughly.

4 Support cylinder with one hand inside, and fold in lower one-third of fabric to form closed bottom of sack.

6 Apply acrylic sealer to entire sack. Paint the sack; to keep fabric from softening, paint inside of sack first and allow it to dry before painting outside. Apply two coats, if necessary. Paint upper edge a contrasting color. Apply acrylic sealer to entire sack.

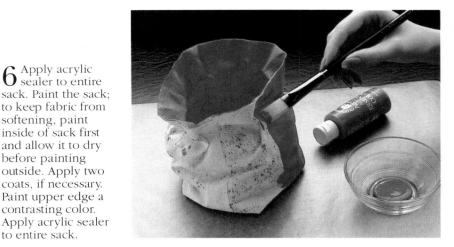

7 Tie cord around sack; glue sprig of greenery over knot, if desired.

1 **Small sack.** Fold over ½" (1.3 cm) on one long edge, and open flat. Dip fabric quickly into cool water; press fold in place. Wipe along all the edges, using a dampened sponge.

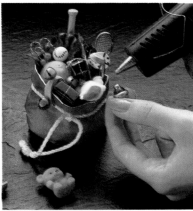

2 Complete the sack, following steps 3 to 7, above. If desired, fill sack with miniature toys and gifts, securing them with hot glue.

FATHER CHRISTMAS

A popular symbol of the holiday season is the legendary Father Christmas. This one is handcrafted from prestarched fabric and is embellished for old-world charm. Prestarched fabric, available at craft stores, is dipped in cool water, then shaped while it is wet, following the tips on page 28. Experiment with samples of prestarched fabric to become familiar with the technique. Oil-based stain, applied to the fabric after it is painted, gives the Father Christmas an antiqued look.

Traditional colors of this Father Christmas are bright and festive. Standing upright, he is holding a small Christmas tree.

Decorator colors from your home may be used instead of the traditional colors. This Father Christmas leans on a walking stick and carries kindling wood.

MATERIALS

- Prestarched fabric, such as Dip 'n Drape®, Drape 'n Shape, or Fab-U-Drape®.
- One 3¼" (8.2 cm) Styrofoam® egg; one 1½" (3.8 cm) Styrofoam ball.
- 12" × 4" (30.5 × 10 cm) Styrofoam cone.
- Floral clay; 18-gauge floral wire; wire cutter.
- Natural or white unspun wool.

- Oil-based stain; 1" (2.5 cm) soft brush.
- Aerosol clear acrylic sealer.
- Acrylic paints; artist's brushes.
- Rubber bands; straight pins; T-pins; craft glue; wax paper; old baking sheet or plastic tray; knife; round toothpicks.
- Hot glue gun and glue sticks.
- Desired accessories.

CUTTING DIRECTIONS

From prestarched fabric, cut one 9" (23 cm) square for the base, one 5" (12.5 cm) square for the face, two 4" (10 cm) squares for the hands, one 14" × 16" (35.5 × 40.5 cm) rectangle for the gown, one 16" × 18" (40.5 × 46 cm) rectangle for the robe, two 6" × 7" (15 × 18 cm) rectangles for the sleeves, one 8" × 13" (20.5 × 33 cm) rectangle for the hood, and one 5" × 7" (12.5 × 18 cm) rectangle for the pouch.

1 Trim ¼" (6 mm) from top of cone, using knife; set aside for the nose. Trim another 1½" (3.8 cm) from top of cone; discard. For Father Christmas with an angled stance, cut a wedge from bottom of the cone, measuring ½" (1.3 cm) on one side and tapering to nothing on opposite side. Wet fabric for base and wrap around bottom of cone; when dry, secure base with floral clay to center of tray. (Extra cone is shown for clarity.)

2 Press center of 3¼" (8.2 cm) Styrofoam egg for head against edge of table; gently roll egg from side to side, creating an indentation halfway around egg.

3 Press with thumbs along edges of indentation to soften cheekline. Roll forehead area lightly on table to soften the line.

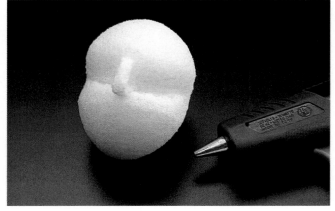

4 Compress sides of Styrofoam reserved for nose into a triangle; soften edges. Turn triangle sideways and glue in place at crest of cheekline, using hot glue.

5 Cut 1½" (3.8 cm) Styrofoam ball in half, using knife. Remove an oblong wedge, measuring ½" × ¾" (1.3 × 2 cm), from one half to form separation between thumb and fingers. Place halves together; cut same shape from other half.

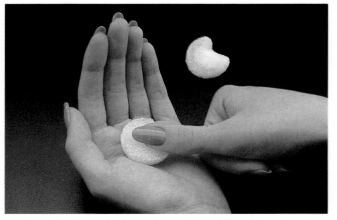

6 Press firmly with finger into palm of Styrofoam hand to make curvature. Soften all cut edges of each hand by rolling on hard, smooth surface and pressing with thumb. Compress Styrofoam for smaller hands.

7 Wet fabric for the face; center over the face, with corners of fabric at top and bottom of the head. Gently pull the side corners of the fabric toward back of head, allowing fabric to cup over features; pull taut over eye area and secure with small pins to prevent wrinkles from occurring when fabric dries. Smooth excess fabric to back of head. Allow to dry on wax paper.

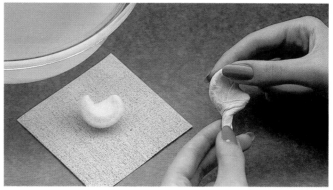

8 Wet fabric for one hand; center over back of hand, with corners at fingertip and wrist areas. Wrap and fold fabric over fingers and press into palm; extend excess fabric down toward wrist area. Keep fabric as smooth as possible on back of hand and between fingers and thumb. Twist fabric at wrist area.

9 Press three parallel lines into back of hand to form fingers, using blade of knife in rocking motion. Repeat for the remaining hand. Allow to dry on wax paper.

10 Apply two coats of acrylic sealer to face and hands; then paint them flesh color. Apply small amount of coral-tone paint to cheeks and nose, blending color. Using pencil, mark placement of eyes, spacing them as indicated in step 11.

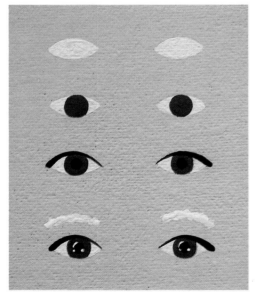

11 Paint eyes and eyebrows as shown. (Photo shows actual size and spacing.)

12 Wet the gown piece. Hand-gather one short side; place on front of cone at the neck, securing with rubber band. Arrange fabric halfway around the cone, turning under raw edge at base. Adjust the folds as necessary, using a T-pin. Place rubber band around cone about 4" (10 cm) from top of cone to define waistline. Allow to dry; remove rubber bands. Apply two coats of acrylic sealer to gown, then paint it desired color.

(Continued)

13 Wet the robe piece. Hand-gather one short side; place on back of cone at neck, securing with rubber band. Turn under sides of robe as they overlap gown piece; turn under the lower raw edges of the robe. Adjust folds as necessary, using a T-pin.

14 Insert two round toothpicks into top of cone, then into base of the head, applying hot glue to secure head to cone.

15 Insert an 18" (46 cm) length of wire through peak of cone, from side to side, for shoulders; secure with hot glue. Shape wire for the shoulders and elbows, with bend of elbows about 3" (7.5 cm) from shoulders. Position wire for arms to hold desired accessories; trim wire so forearm and upper arm are same length.

16 Push wire into Styrofoam at back of hand near wrist; secure wire with hot glue.

17 Fold ½" (1.3 cm) hem on one short side of sleeve piece; unfold. Wet fabric, refold hem, and fold fabric for elbow. Form sleeve loosely around arm, overlapping hand slightly. Close sleeve at hand to conceal wire; hand-gather fabric at neck. Adjust folds as necessary, using a T-pin; pull fabric away from cone to create shoulder line.

18 Fold ½" (1.3 cm) hem on one long side of hood piece; unfold. Wet fabric, and refold hem. Place hood on head with hemmed edge around face; turn under front corners of hood, pinning in place with T-pins. Stuff small amount of wax paper between hood and top of head to allow space for hair.

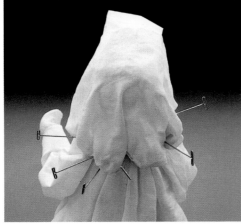

19 Turn under the raw edge at back of hood; pin in place. Remove pins and wax paper when hood is dry.

20 Wet the pouch fabric; place on wax paper. Fold a paper towel into 2" (5 cm) square. Fold long sides of fabric over paper towel. Fold in opposite ends, inserting 16" (40.5 cm) length of cording; shape top of pouch into rounded flap. Allow to dry.

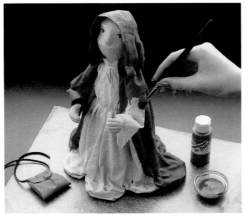

21 Apply two coats of acrylic sealer to robe and pouch. Paint them desired color; paint inside edges of hood and sleeves. Allow to dry.

22 Apply two coats of acrylic sealer to Father Christmas and pouch. Apply the stain, using an old brush. When items are completely covered with stain, wipe off excess with clean rag, leaving the stain in the recessed areas to maintain dark contrast. If the stain reappears while drying, rewipe as necessary. Allow to dry thoroughly.

23 Arrange wool for desired effect for hair, beard, and moustache; glue in place, using hot glue.

24 Drape pouch over shoulder, tying ends together. Attach a belt and additional accessories, securing them with hot glue. Apply light coat of acrylic sealer for protective finish.

WINTER VILLAGE

Memories of old can be captured in this small re-creation of a winter village. A fascination for children and adults, this village is aglow with its own lighting. The buildings get their basic shape from milk cartons and can be crafted to achieve a variety of exterior finishes. The village can be accessorized with any quarter-scale figures and embellishments and can be displayed with a model train.

HOW TO MAKE A CAPE COD COTTAGE

MATERIALS

- 1-qt. (0.9 L) milk carton.
- Balsa or bass wood: ⅛" (3 mm) clapboard siding; corner molding; ¹⁄₁₆" × ¼" (1.5 × 6 mm) strips for shingles and shutters; ¹⁄₁₆" × ⅛" (1.5 × 3 mm) flat trim for gable; wood board, ¹⁄₁₆" (1.5 mm) thick, for door; wood strip, ⅛" (3 mm) thick, for steps.
- Acrylic paints; artist's brushes.
- Clear plastic film and ¹⁄₃₂" (0.8 mm) white graphic chart tape for windows.
- Sculpey® or Fimo® polymer clay for chimney; small bead for doorknob.
- Masking tape; fine sandpaper; metal straightedge; mat knife.
- Thick craft glue; hot glue gun and glue sticks.

1 Open top of milk carton; cut out areas as shown. Mark lines on all sides of carton 2" (5 cm) from top foldline of carton; cut on marked lines.

2 Tape top and sides of carton together to form gables, trimming upper edges of top as necessary so edges meet at peak. Sand all sides lightly.

(Continued)

3 Cut two pieces for roof from remainder of carton, each measuring 2⅜" × 3⅛" (6.2 × 7.8 cm); tape pieces together along long side. Sand roof pieces lightly. Cut 1/16" × ¼" (1.5 × 6 mm) balsa into ⅜" (1 cm) lengths, using mat knife. Cut a few pieces in half lengthwise to use as needed at ends of rows.

4 Glue shingles in place on roof, starting at bottom edges, using thick craft glue; bottom rows should overhang the roof ⅛" (3 mm). Continue to glue rows of shingles up to top of each piece, staggering shingles and overlapping rows ⅛" (3 mm).

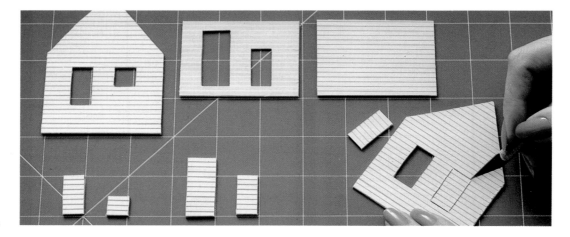

5 Trace shape of walls and gable on the back of the clapboard siding; cut pieces, using mat knife and metal straightedge. Cut openings in siding for windows and doors as desired, cutting the door ¼" (6 mm) from the bottom edge, to allow room for steps.

6 Glue siding on house, using hot glue. Cut the corner moldings to fit the corners of the house; glue in place. Cut out milk carton in window areas; for the door, cut along three sides and fold on remaining side. Paint the house as desired, using an acrylic paint.

7 Cut the shutters and door from 1/16" (1.5 mm) balsa wood; paint, and glue in place. Glue small bead in place for doorknob.

8 Cut clear plastic film slightly larger than each window. Outline windows and make mullions with graphic chart tape. Tape windows in place from inside of box, using masking tape.

9 Cut two ¹⁄₁₆" × (1.5 × 6 mm) strips of balsa wood to the length of roof top. Paint roof and strips with thinned acrylic paint so wood grain shows through; paint edges on the underside of roof. Weight roof while drying to prevent warping.

10 Glue the roof in place. Glue the strips of balsa wood to the length of roof top over top rows of shingles. Cut flat trim to fit peak; paint and glue in place.

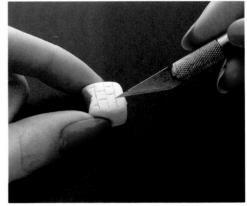

11 Shape polymer clay into chimney shape, cutting bottom of chimney to fit roof. Use mat knife to score brick pattern on chimney.

12 Bake the chimney, following the manufacturer's instructions. Paint chimney, and glue to roof.

13 Cut one ¾" × ¾" (2 × 2 cm) and one ½" × ¾" (1.3 × 2 cm) piece from ⅛" (3 mm) wood; glue together for steps. Paint as desired; glue in place beneath door.

VARIATIONS FOR VILLAGE HOUSES

To add variety to the winter village, the sizes and shapes of some of the houses may be changed. Stucco and brick may be used for the exterior finishes instead of clapboard siding. Asphalt and wood-shingle roofs may be used on some of the houses instead of wood shakes.

HOW TO VARY THE SIZE & SHAPE OF HOUSES

Tape portions of cartons together for houses of various sizes and shapes. To add dormers, use the pattern on page 124. Vary the exterior finishes, as shown below and opposite.

HOW TO MAKE A STUCCO EXTERIOR

Apply one or two coats of artificial snow paste to the sides of the house after the windows and doors have been cut.

HOW TO MAKE A BRICK EXTERIOR

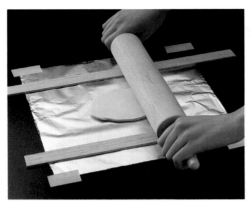

1 Roll polymer clay on a sheet of heavy aluminum foil to ⅛" (3 mm) thickness; to ensure even thickness, support sides of rolling pin with ⅛" (3 mm) strips of wood.

2 Mark the dimensions of house on clay. Cut on marked lines, using mat knife; do not cut through foil. Remove excess clay. Mark placement of doors and windows by scoring the clay. Score clay, marking horizontal rows ⅛" (3 mm) apart; score clay vertically for individual bricks.

3 Cut out doors and windows. Transfer the foil to a baking sheet, and bake according to manufacturer's instructions.

4 Glue the brick pieces to sides of house, using hot glue. Cut out doors and windows in milk carton. Glue corner moldings at corners of house. Paint the brick and moldings desired color.

HOW TO MAKE WOOD-SHINGLE & ASPHALT ROOFS

Wood-shingle roof. Mark roof measurements from carton on back of ¼" (6 mm) clapboard; add ⅜" (1 cm) width and length for overhangs and eaves. Cut pieces, using mat knife and metal straightedge. Cut corner molding the length of roof. Paint roof and corner molding with thinned paint. Mark staggered lines for shingles, using mat knife. Weight roof while drying to prevent warping. Glue roof in place. Glue corner molding along roof top.

Asphalt roof. Cut #60 coarse sandpaper into ¼" (6 mm) strips; from strips, cut ¼" × ⅜" (6 mm × 1 cm) shingles. Cut a few pieces in half lengthwise to use as needed at ends of rows. Attach shingles as on page 102, step 4. Fold ¼" (6 mm) strip of sandpaper in half; glue in place over top rows of shingles.

VILLAGE CHURCH

A red brick church, with its bell tower, pillared entryway, and stained glass windows, is an important part of the village. The basic construction of the church is the same as for the houses on page 101.

MATERIALS

- Three 1-qt. (0.9 L) milk cartons.
- Balsa or bass wood: 1/8" (3 mm) clapboard for siding of tower; 1/4" (6 mm) clapboard for roof; corner molding for corners of church and top of roof; 1/16" × 1/8" (1.5 × 3 mm) flat trim for gable and tower back; wood strip, 3/16" (4.5 mm) thick, for steps; wood strip, 1/16" (1.5 mm) thick, for doors; dowel, for pillars.
- 6 oz. (170 g) Sculpey® polymer clay for brick; aluminum foil; rolling pin; baking sheet.
- Acrylic paints; artist's brushes; clear plastic film; 1/32" (0.8 mm) black graphic chart tape; stained glass paints or permanent marking pens.
- Two small beads for doorknobs; small bell and bead for steeple.
- Masking tape; fine sandpaper; thick craft glue; hot glue gun and glue sticks; mat knife.

HOW TO MAKE A VILLAGE CHURCH

1 Follow steps 1 and 2 on page 101, marking the lines 3½" (9 cm) from top foldline; repeat for second carton. Tape the two cartons together securely.

2 Cut piece for bell tower, 6½" high × 5" wide (16.3 × 12.5 cm), from remaining carton; position fold of carton on the lengthwise center of rectangle. Mark and score a line 1¼" (3.2 cm) from each long edge.

3 Fold tower, and tape together. Cut piece for steeple from carton, using pattern on page 124; score on dotted lines. Fold steeple, and tape together.

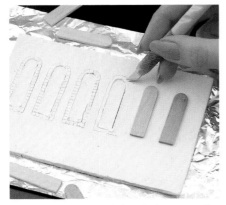

4 Make and attach brick (page 105) to sides of church, using a 1½" (3.8 cm) portion of popsicle stick for window pattern; if desired, score brick around windows as shown.

5 Make and attach windows as on page 103, step 8, using black chart tape. If desired, paint windows, using stained glass paints or permanent marking pens.

6 Attach wood-shingle roof (page 105). Paint flat trim, and glue to front and back of church, with lower edge 3½" (9 cm) from bottom of church; cut ends to fit roof angle. Cut flat trim for peak; paint, and glue in place.

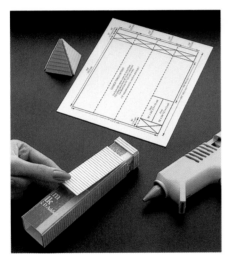

7 Cut clapboard and doors for the tower and steeple according to patterns on pages 124 and 125. Glue clapboard in place, using hot glue.

8 Cut corner moldings to fit corners of tower and steeple; glue in place. Cut away carton for windows. Cut flat trim, and attach to top and bottom of windows. Cut two 3½" (9 cm) strips of flat trim; attach to back of tower at bottom of corner moldings.

9 Paint tower and steeple. Score roof for shingles, if desired. Attach bell to a length of wire, and insert wire through top of steeple; adjust height of bell, and glue in place. Trim excess wire. Glue steeple to tower; glue bead at peak of steeple.

10 Paint and attach the doors, with lower edge ⅝" (1.5 cm) from bottom of tower. Glue beads for doorknobs in place. Cut one 1½" × 1½" (3.8 × 3.8 cm) piece, one 1¼" × 1½" (3.2 × 3.8 cm), and one 1" × 1½" (2.5 × 3.8 cm) from ³⁄₁₆" (4.5 mm) wood; glue together for steps. Paint the steps as desired, and glue in place.

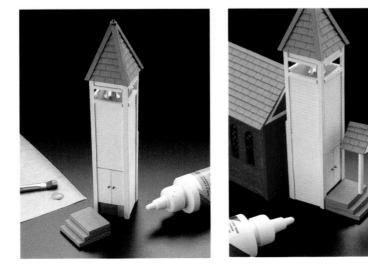

11 Cut two 1" (2.5 cm) squares from the clapboard for the awning roof; cut awning front, using pattern on page 124. Glue awning pieces together; paint. Score roof for shingles, if desired. Cut two pillars from dowel, each 1¾" (4.5 cm) long; paint. Glue awning and pillars in place; position pillars on top step. Glue tower to front of church.

TIPS FOR LANDSCAPING THE VILLAGE

Landscape base. Cut foam board to desired size. Wrap the board with polyester fleece or quilt batting; tape in place on underside.

Skating pond. Cut away the fleece or batting to desired shape of skating pond. Apply sheet of silver Mylar® to foam board, using spray adhesive. Use white paint pen to simulate tracings from skate blades, if desired.

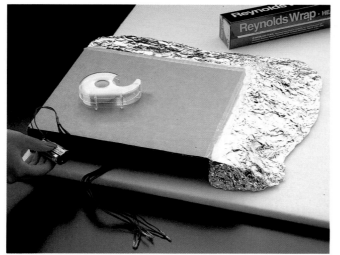

1 Hill. Shape a hill, using a box and crumpled foil. Battery packs for lighting can be stored in box.

2 Cover hill with fleece or batting. Add small stones or polymer clay stones (opposite), moss, and twigs as desired; attach, using hot glue.

1 Lighting. Use battery-operated lights, concealing battery packs in hill (above). Cut slit in fleece or batting; run wiring to buildings.

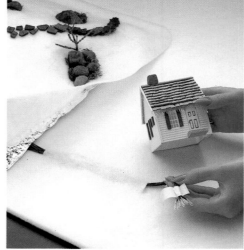

2 Cluster light bulbs; tape together. Tape to ceiling inside house.

Hedges and shrubs.
Use sprigs of artificial garland for hedges. For the shrubs, wind the garland sprigs around finger, or trim the tops from miniature pine trees, using wire cutter.

Stonework. Roll polymer clay to ⅛" (3 mm) thickness; use a toothpick to form stones in clay. Bake clay, following the manufacturer's instructions; paint as desired. Place the stonework on fleece or batting to create walkways.

Snow and icicles.
Sprinkle artificial snow to conceal lighting wires and add finishing touch to roofs, hedges, and other items. Glue purchased icicles designed for miniature villages to the eaves of the buildings.

Gift
Wrapping

KEEPSAKE GIFT BOXES

For memorable gift giving, create spectacular packages. The gift boxes themselves can become keepsakes for storing mementos like your favorite Christmas cards and letters. Or they may be used again for wrapping next year's presents.

Bandboxes can be transformed into gift boxes that resemble antiqued drums. Or use wicker baskets with lids as gift boxes; embellished with special trims, the baskets themselves become an extra gift.

Decoupaged boxes, embellished with cutouts from special Christmas cards, antique reproduction cutouts, and metallic trims have old-fashioned appeal. The beautifully wrapped boxes are preserved for years to come by applying a decoupage medium to the wrapping paper. For best results, use sturdy, noncollapsible gift boxes and wrapping papers that are heavier in weight. Lightweight papers can be strengthened by spraying them with aerosol clear acrylic sealer. For shallow boxes, it may only be necessary to cover the lid of the box. On deeper boxes with shallow lids, cover both the box and the lid.

Paper lace fans can adorn decoupaged gift boxes for a dimensional effect. For easier storage of gift boxes with paper lace fans, make the fans detachable by using self-adhesive hook and loop tape.

HOW TO MAKE A DRUM GIFT BOX

MATERIALS

- Wooden bandbox; extra lid from a second bandbox, optional.
- Acrylic paints; oil-based stain; artist's brushes.
- Braids and trims to simulate detailing of drums.
- Craft glue.
- Two large wooden beads and two wooden dowels to fit into beads, for drumsticks; length of dowels depends on diameter of bandbox lid.

1 Glue extra lid, if desired, on bottom of box. Glue wooden bead to one end of each dowel to make drumsticks; allow to dry. Paint bandbox and drumsticks. When dry, apply stain, following manufacturer's instructions.

2 Glue trim to sides of box to simulate detailing of drum. Glue drumsticks in place on top of lid. Glue braid to lower edge of box and upper edge of lid; cover ends of braid with a trim for a neater finish.

HOW TO MAKE A BASKET GIFT BOX

MATERIALS

- Wicker basket with lid.
- Acrylic paint and oil-based stain, if desired; artist's brushes.
- Craft glue.
- Embellishments as desired, such as dried naturals or miniatures.

1 Apply paint and stain to wicker basket, if desired.

2 Embellish gift box as desired; secure items with hot glue.

HOW TO MAKE A DECOUPAGE GIFT BOX

MATERIALS

- Gift boxes.
- Wrapping paper.
- Decoupage medium; brush or sponge applicator.
- Metallic or pearlescent acrylic paint, optional.
- Embellishments as desired, such as dried naturals, decorative cutouts, ribbons, braids, doilies, and glitter glue.

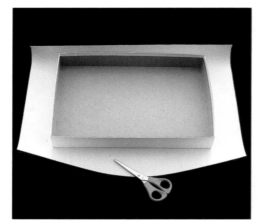

1 Cut wrapping paper so it extends 1" to 2" (2.5 to 5 cm) beyond the edges of the box or lid.

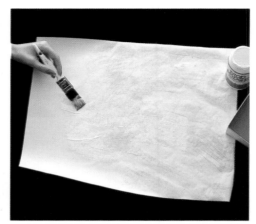

2 Spread decoupage medium on the wrong side of the wrapping paper; allow to set about 1 minute to prevent paper from bubbling when mounted.

3 Center the box or lid on the wrong side of wrapping paper. Turn over, and smooth the paper in place, removing any bubbles.

4 Turn box over, and smooth paper onto two long sides. Cut paper from upper edge to corner; wrap paper to inside of box. Trim remaining paper at sides even with edge of box.

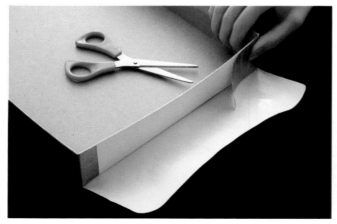

5 Cut paper at ends into the corner; fold flaps, trimming excess paper, if desired. Secure the flaps to the short sides of the box.

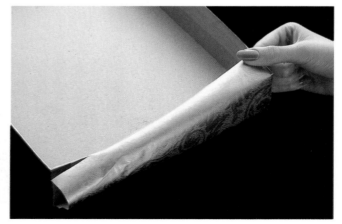

6 Smooth paper in place on short sides of box and around to inside. Allow box to dry thoroughly.

7 Use decoupage medium to affix embellishments, such as cutouts, to box; allow to dry.

8 Highlight the cutouts with glitter glue or with pearlescent or metallic paint, if desired; apply paint with brush and circular strokes, or dab paint on with small piece of natural sponge.

9 Brush a thin coat of decoupage medium onto entire outside surface; allow to dry. Additional coats may be applied, if desired; to eliminate brush strokes, sand lightly between coats, using fine sandpaper.

10 Apply heavier trims, such as dried naturals, with craft glue. Apply acrylic sealer.

HOW TO MAKE A PAPER FAN GIFT BOX

MATERIALS

- Gift boxes.
- Wrapping paper.
- Decoupage medium; brush or sponge applicator.
- Circles of light-duty hook and loop tape.
- Materials for paper fans, listed on page 19.
- Ribbon for bow, if desired.

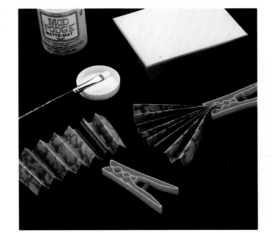

1 Make decoupage box, following steps 1 to 6, opposite, and step 9, above. Make paper fans as on page 19.

2 Secure loop side of hook and loop tape to bottom edges of paper fans and bow; secure hook side to package.

VICTORIAN CARDS

Paper doilies, either round or square, can be folded and embellished to create unique cards, gifts tags, and package trims. For an old-fashioned look, use antique reproduction cutouts and stickers, available in stationery stores and gift shops. Or create your own cutouts from Christmas cards and wrapping paper. Decorative doilies and medallions are available from stationery stores and cake decorating suppliers.

MATERIALS

- Round paper doilies in 8", 10", or 12" (20.5, 25.5, or 30.5 cm) sizes.
- Square paper doilies in 8" or 10" (20.5 or 25.5 cm) sizes; doilies should have solid square area at center.
- Cutouts or stickers.
- Glue stick.
- Embellishments as desired, such as ribbon, feathers, foil leaves and medallions, foil papers, and glitter glue.

FOUR WAYS TO FOLD VICTORIAN CARDS

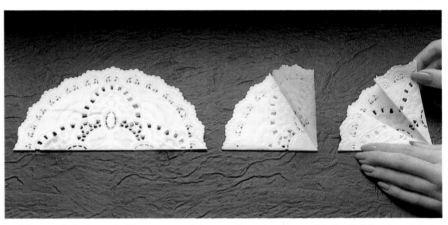

Fold round doily in half, wrong sides together; then fold right and left sides so edges meet in center.

Fold round doily in half, wrong sides together, then into thirds. Fold outer thirds in half so folded edges meet in center.

Fold opposite corners of square doily along solid area. Fold back points, if desired, so folded edges meet.

Fold all four corners of square doily along solid area, envelope-style.

GIFT WRAPPING
117

Glue 6" to 8" (15 to 20.5 cm) lengths of silk ribbon to doily, with glued ends facing away from center, for ties. Glue cutout, which has been cut in half, on doily over ribbons.

Strengthen wrapping paper by spraying four or five coats of acrylic sealer on both sides. Cut design from wrapping paper; glue to doily.

Cut decorative foil paper, and glue in center of square doily for colorful background under motif.

Embellish cards with gold leaves and medallions, gluing them in place. Or add small stickers to cards.

Create pop-up designs by mounting them on heavy strips of paper, folded into M or Z shapes.

Highlight designs with glitter.

Sign the card on a small "banner" of paper or ribbon. Or add gift tags to the embellishments.

Glue medallions or portions of doilies under cutout motifs for added interest. Tuck feathers behind designs, if desired.

MORE IDEAS FOR GIFT WRAPPING

Embossed gift cards *are made using a stamp and embossing ink and powder. Cut around the top portion of the design with a mat knife, if desired, before folding the gift card.*

Gift bags *can be personalized with appliqués cut from fabric and applied with spray adhesive. Perforated bags designed for use with candles may also be used for gift bags.*

Ornaments, *used instead of bows, become an extra keepsake gift. This package is embellished with a lace nosegay ornament (page 21).*

Santa sacks *(page 92) make creative packaging for gifts of food or plants.*

Stamps *can be used to create your own wrapping paper. Use permanent marking pens to add detailing to the stamped designs.*

Tassels and medallions *add an elegant touch to tailored bows.*

Creative napkin rings *(page 58) can decorate the neck of a bottle or the handle of a basket.*

Small artificial wreath, *cut and attached to the rim of a gift basket, adds a festive touch.*

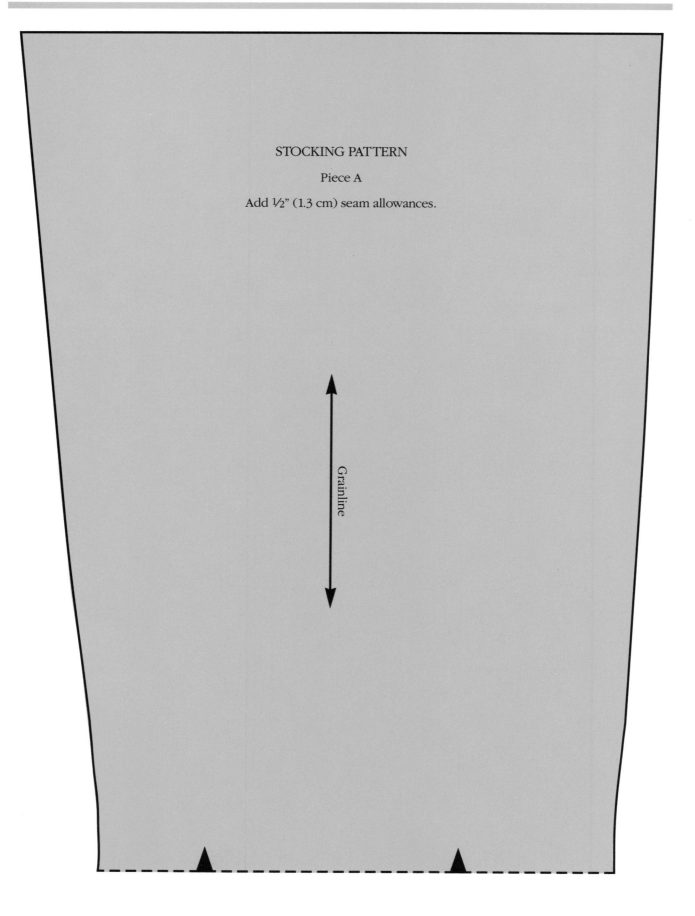

STOCKING PATTERN

Piece A

Add ½" (1.3 cm) seam allowances.

Grainline

STOCKING PATTERN

Piece B

Add ½" (1.3 cm) seam allowances.

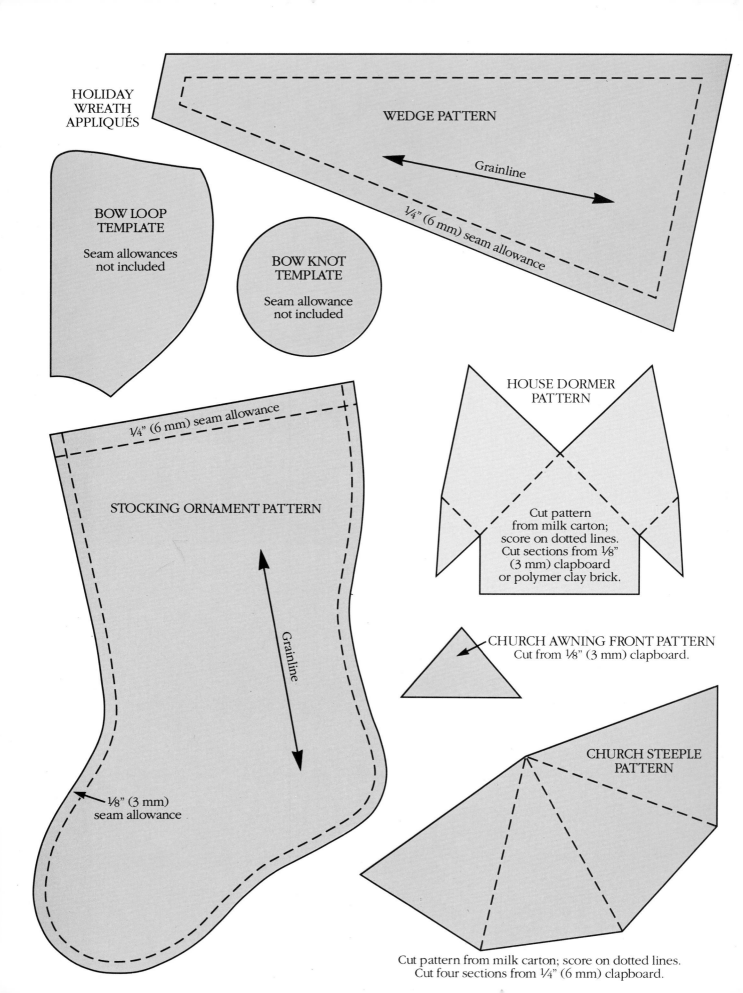

HOLIDAY
WREATH
APPLIQUÉS

WEDGE PATTERN

Grainline

¼" (6 mm) seam allowance

BOW LOOP
TEMPLATE

Seam allowances
not included

BOW KNOT
TEMPLATE

Seam allowance
not included

HOUSE DORMER
PATTERN

¼" (6 mm) seam allowance

STOCKING ORNAMENT PATTERN

Grainline

Cut pattern
from milk carton;
score on dotted lines.
Cut sections from ⅛"
(3 mm) clapboard
or polymer clay brick.

CHURCH AWNING FRONT PATTERN
Cut from ⅛" (3 mm) clapboard.

⅛" (3 mm)
seam allowance

CHURCH STEEPLE
PATTERN

Cut pattern from milk carton; score on dotted lines.
Cut four sections from ¼" (6 mm) clapboard.

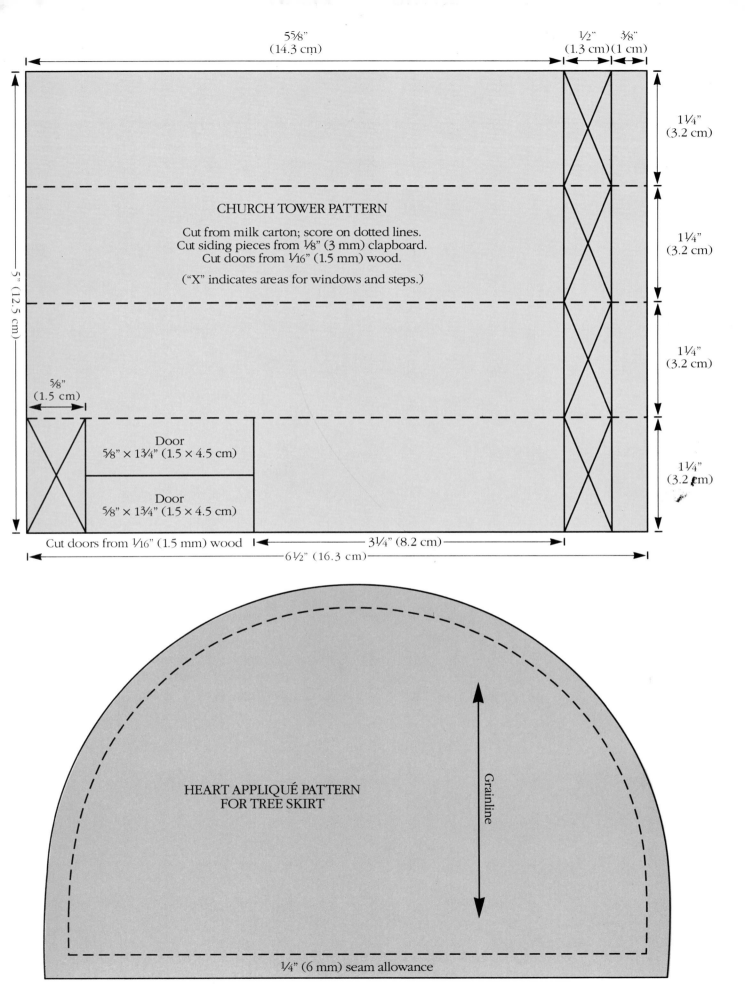

55⁄8"
(14.3 cm)

1⁄2"
(1.3 cm)

3⁄8"
(1 cm)

1¼"
(3.2 cm)

CHURCH TOWER PATTERN

Cut from milk carton; score on dotted lines.
Cut siding pieces from 1⁄8" (3 mm) clapboard.
Cut doors from 1⁄16" (1.5 mm) wood.

("X" indicates areas for windows and steps.)

1¼"
(3.2 cm)

5" (12.5 cm)

1¼"
(3.2 cm)

5⁄8"
(1.5 cm)

Door
5⁄8" × 1¾" (1.5 × 4.5 cm)

Door
5⁄8" × 1¾" (1.5 × 4.5 cm)

1¼"
(3.2 cm)

Cut doors from 1⁄16" (1.5 mm) wood

3¼" (8.2 cm)

6½" (16.3 cm)

HEART APPLIQUÉ PATTERN
FOR TREE SKIRT

Grainline

¼" (6 mm) seam allowance

INDEX

A

Angel, treetop, 9-10
Angel ornament, lace, 15-16
Appliqués,
  heart, 38
  holiday wreath, 44-45
  patterns for, 124-125
Artificial garland centerpiece, 56-57

B

Bags, gift, 120
Ball ornaments,
  lace, 20-21
  plastic and glass, 20-23, 30-31
  potpourri, 18-19
Bannisters, garlands for, 70, 73
Basket gift box, 113
Bow templates, 124
Bows, 74-77
  templates for, 124
  to trim trees, 11-12, 32-33
Box, gift, centerpiece, 54-55
Boxes, keepsake gift, 113-115
Braid-trimmed placemats, 46, 49
Bridal illusion, to trim trees, 33

C

Cape Cod cottages, 101-105
Cards,
  embossed gift, 120
  Victorian, 117-119
Centerpieces, 54-57
Church, for winter village, 106-107
  patterns for, 124-125
Cinnamon sticks, as ornaments, 30-31
Clay, polymer,
  also see: snowman ornament, winter
    village
  tips for shaping, 26
Clothespins, as ornaments, 31
Cluster bows, 74-75, 77
  as tree topper, 11-12
Cone trees, 84-87
Contrasting mitered bands,
  on placemats, 46, 48
  on table runners, 42-43
Cottages, Cape Cod, 101-105
Crazy quilting, on tree skirts, 39
Crazy-quilt stockings, 78-79, 81-82

D

Decoupage gift box, 113-115
Doilies,
  crocheted, for treetop angel, 9-10
  lace, for ornaments, 15-17, 20-21
  paper, for Victorian cards, 116-119
Double topiary trees, 91
Dried naturals,
  for cone trees, 84-87
  for topiary trees, 90-91
  as tree toppers, 11
  for wreaths, 66, 68
Dried rosebuds,
  as ornaments, 30
  for topiary trees, 91
Dried-natural cone tree, 84, 86-87
Drum gift box, 112-113
Drum ornament, 28-29

E

Embossed gift cards, 120
Ensembles, table, 60-61
Etched glassware, 59
Eucalyptus wreath, 64-65, 68
Evergreen spray centerpiece, 56-57
Evergreen wreath, fresh, 64-65

F

Fabric, prestarched,
  for drum ornament, 28-29
  for Father Christmas, 94-99
  for Santa sacks, 92-93
  tips for using, 28
Fabric-wrapped ornaments, 22, 25
Fan gift box, paper, 112-113, 115
Fan ornament, paper, 18-19
Father Christmas, 94-99
Filled ornaments, 22-23
  as centerpiece, 56
Fireplaces, garlands for, 72-73
French ribbon bows, 74-75

G

Garland centerpiece, 56-57
Garland sprig napkin rings, 58-59
Garlands, 70-73

Gift

Gift bags, 120
Gift box centerpiece, 54-55
Gift boxes, keepsake, 112-115
Gift cards, embossed, 120
Gift wrapping, ideas for, 120-121
Gilded ornaments, 22-25
Glass and plastic ornaments,
  decorated, 20-24, 30-31
Glassware, etched, 59

H

Heart appliqués,
  pattern for, 125
  for tree skirts, 35, 38
Holiday wreath appliqués,
  for placemats, 46-47, 51
  for table runners, 42-44
  templates for, 124
  for tree skirts, 34-35
Houses, for winter village, 100-105
  dormer pattern, 124

K

Keepsake gift boxes, 112-115

L

Lace napkin rings, 58-59
Lace ornaments, 14-17, 20-21
Landscaping a winter village, 108-109
Lemon cone tree, 84-85
Lined stockings, 78-80
Lined tree skirts, 35, 37, 39
Linens, table, painted, 52-53, 61

M

Medallions, for gift wrapping, 121
Mitered hems,
  on placemats, 46, 48
  on table runners, 42-43

CREDITS

CY DECOSSE INCORPORATED

A  COWLES MAGAZINES COMPANY

Chairman/CEO: Bruce Barnet
Chairman Emeritus: Cy DeCosse
President/COO: Nino Tarantino
Executive V.P./Editor-in-Chief:
William B. Jones

DECORATING FOR CHRISTMAS
Created by: The Editors of
Cy DeCosse Incorporated

Also available from the publisher:
*Bedroom Decorating, Creative
Window Treatments, Decorating the
Living Room, Creative Accessories
for the Home, Decorating with Silk
& Dried Flowers, Decorating the
Kitchen, Kitchen & Bathroom Ideas,
Decorative Painting, Decorating your
Home for Christmas, Decorating for
Dining & Entertaining, Decorating
with Fabric & Wallcovering,
Decorating the Bathroom*

Executive Editor: Zoe A. Graul
Technical Director: Rita C. Opseth
Project Manager: Linda S. Halls

Senior Art Director: Delores Swanson
Writer: Rita C. Opseth
Editor: Janice Cauley
Sample Coordinator: Carol Olson
Technical Photo Director: Bridget
Haugh
Photo Stylists: Patrice Dingmann,
Coralie Sathre
Styling Director: Bobbette Destiche
Crafts Stylist: Joanne Wawra
Research Assistant: Lori Ritter
Artisans: Jann Erickson, Susan Frame,
Phyllis Galbraith, Bridget Haugh, Sara
Macdonald, Linda Neubauer, Carol
Olson, Carol Pilot, Nancy Sundeen,
Barbara Teerlinck
*Director of Development Planning
& Production:* Jim Bindas
Photo Studio Manager: Cathleen
Shannon
Lead Photographer: Mark Macemon
Photographers: Rex Irmen, John
Lauenstein, Bill Lindner, Paul Najlis,
Mette Nielsen, Mike Parker
Contributing Photographers: Phil
Aarestad, Kim Bailey, Paul Herda,
Charles Nields, Brad Parker, Marc
Scholtes
Production Manager: Amelia Merz
Production Staff: Diane Dreon-Krattiger,
Adam Esco, Joe Fahey, Peter Gloege,

Eva Hanson, Jeff Hickman, Paul Najlis,
Mike Schauer, Linda Schloegel, Rena
Tassone, Nik Wogstad
Scenic Carpenters: Tom Cooper, Jim
Huntley, Phil Juntti, Greg Wallace,
Wayne Wendland
Consultants: Carol Duvall, Wendy Fedie,
Margot Ketz, Kristi Kuhnau, Diane
Schultz, Sue Stein, Barbara Teerlinck,
Donna Whitman
Contributors: Hamilton Adams Imports
Ltd.; Armour Products; C. M. Offray &
Son, Inc.; Coats & Clark Inc.; Concord
House, Division of Concord Fabrics Inc.;
Conso Products Company; Decart Inc.;
Dritz Corporation; Dyno Merchandise
Corporation; Marvin Windows, Inc.; The
Singer Company; Swiss-Metrosene, Inc.;
Wamsutta OTC/Division of Springs
Industries, Inc.
Printed on American paper by:
Quebecor Graphics (0695)

Cy DeCosse Incorporated offers a variety of
how-to books. For information write:
Cy DeCosse Subscriber Books
5900 Green Oak Drive
Minnetonka, MN 55343